CULTURES OF THE WORLD
Zambia

Cavendish
Square
New York

Published in 2014 by Cavendish Square Publishing, LLC
Published in 2018 by Cavendish Square Publishing, LLC
243 5th Avenue, Suite 136, New York, NY 10016
Copyright © 2018 by Cavendish Square Publishing, LLC

Third Edition

Library of Congress Cataloging-in-Publication Data

Names: Holmes, Timothy, 1936- author. | Wong, Winnie, author. | Nevins, Debbie, author.
Title: Zambia / Timothy Holmes, Winnie Wong, Debbie Nevins. |
Description: Third edition. | New York : Cavendish Square Publishing, 2018. |
Series: Cultures of the world (third edition) | Includes bibliographical references and index. | Audience: Grades 5-8.
Identifiers: LCCN 2017044406 (print) | LCCN 2017045837 (ebook) | ISBN 9781502632432 (library bound) | ISBN 9781502632449 (eBook)
Subjects: LCSH: Zambia--Juvenile literature.
Classification: LCC DT3042 (ebook) | LCC DT3042 .H64 2017 (print) | DDC 968.94--dc23
LC record available at https://lccn.loc.gov/2017044406

Writers, Timothy Holmes, Winnie Wong; Debbie Nevins, third edition
Editorial Director, third edition: David McNamara
Editor, third edition: Debbie Nevins
Art Director, third edition: Amy Greenan
Designer, third edition: Jessica Nevins
Picture Researcher, third edition: Jessica Nevins

PRECEDING PAGE
The waters of the Zambezi cascade over the edge of Victoria Falls.

Printed in the United States of America

CONTENTS

ZAMBIA TODAY

Z **AMBIA IS A BEAUTIFUL, LARGE COUNTRY IN SOUTH CENTRAL** Africa. It's a land where lions roam grassy plains, elephants plod through verdant bush, and hippos bathe in the great Zambezi River. It's a land where termites build sandcastles to the sky, and the rainy time of year is called the "Emerald Season," because everything turns so green. Vast, remote stretches of wilderness provide astonishing vistas and a rich diversity of wildlife.

Although it's a landlocked country—meaning it has no coastline—Zambia has a wealth of water in its many rivers and lakes. There are at least eighteen spectacular waterfalls, some of them in such remote areas that there's no road leading to them. For hardier tourists, willing to hike to secluded places, waterfall tours are becoming a popular attraction. The greatest of the falls, however, is easily seen in the southern town of Livingstone. Victoria Falls on the Zambezi River, which marks the border between Zambia and Zimbabwe, is not only Africa's grandest waterfall, but it is known as the greatest curtain of falling water in the world. Mosi-oa-Tunya ("The Smoke that Thunders"), as it is also called, lives up to its name.

Lions rest in the shade at South Luangwa National Park in Zambia.

Nature is a national treasure in Zambia. Another is the Zambian people themselves. Most are descendants of the indigenous Bantu-speaking tribes who lived in this region for centuries, and they have kept their traditional culture alive against great odds. Many of today's Zambians remain loyal to their tribal chiefs, successors of the precolonial African kings, even as they are patriotic, voting members of the modern state.

Zambia wasn't always Zambia. From 1911 to 1964, it was Northern Rhodesia, a colony of the British Empire; and before that, from 1889, it was a British-controlled protectorate. The British—and others—wanted the region for the rich band of copper that extends beneath its surface. Prior to its dominance by the Europeans, this land, like much of interior Africa, was a loose conglomeration of small indigenous kingdoms. The old ways rooted in that distant past are celebrated with colorful festivals and traditional rituals.

This is the legendary Africa—the wild and noble Africa that fires the imagination. And though this vision is true and real, it's far from the full picture. Like many African nations, Zambia is a very poor country. The statistics are shocking. According to the World Food Programme (WFP), 60 percent of people in Zambia live below the poverty line and 42 percent are considered to be extremely poor. People are hungry, and children are malnourished. Some 53 percent of children under five years of age are anemic, and 40 percent are stunted from insufficient nutrients. Newborns and toddlers die at an alarming rate—75 out of 1,000 each year in 2014—and that's an improvement over the past!

Zambia, like many other sub-Saharan nations, has been ravaged by the HIV/AIDS epidemic. This scourge has killed so many adults in recent years that one out of every five children is an orphan—that's about 1.5 million children who have lost their parents. A very poor country cannot sustain such loss without it severely impacting its present and future.

Adding to the nation's woes—and perhaps a not surprising consequence of them—is the political upheaval that beset the government in the past decade or so. A crisis of leadership in 2009 put a halt to the economic growth that had been sparking some hope. Although stability appears to have returned with the election of Edgar Lungu in 2016, some observers are voicing concerns about a drift toward authoritarianism. It's too soon to tell at this writing, and in fragile nations, political fortunes can turn quickly.

HIV/AIDS educators talk to orphans at a school run by the Society for Women and AIDS in Zambia.

The good news is that Zambia remains a reasonably steady democratic country. It is not a failed state. Unlike some of its war-torn neighbors, it has not succumbed to civil war. Its various ethnic and religious groups get along pretty well.

So why is Zambia so poor? The list of culprits is long, complex, and intertwined—starting with colonialism and its inherent racism. Mining and foreign exploitation, political and corporate corruption; pollution, deforestation, and soil degradation; a culture of gender inequality, early marriage, and a high birthrate; the devastation of HIV/AIDS on the population; a lack of a skilled labor force; insufficient infrastructure, jobs, education, and health services—the list goes on. Essentially Zambia is poor because it is so very poor. It's a knotty puzzle that the Zambian government, along with many international organizations, from the African Union to CARE International to the United States African Development Foundation, are trying to solve.

GEOGRAPHY

A tree overlooks Zambia's Lake Bangweulu. The name means "Where the water meets the sky."

LANDLOCKED IN SUBSAHARAN Africa, Zambia is a large country of extraordinary beauty. Sprawling across the plateau of south-central Africa, it is 290,586 square miles (752,614 square km) in extent, which makes it slightly larger than Texas. Zambia has no coastline, but it has quite a few neighbors. To the south, it borders Zimbabwe, Botswana, and Namibia; to the east, Tanzania, Malawi, and Mozambique; the Democratic Republic of Congo to the north; and Angola to the west.

The Zambian Plateau lies about 3,000 feet (966 meters) above sea level. There are no real mountains, but the highest point (8,503 feet/2,592 m) is an unnamed location in the Mafinga Hills. The most distinctive features of the landscape are the deep gorges and valleys of the lower Zambezi and Luangwa Rivers. Their precipitous escarpments look like mountains from below. These troughs are limbs of the Great African Rift Valley, which extends from Mozambique to the Red Sea.

Zambia takes its name from the magnificent Zambezi River, which rises in the country's North-Western Province near the border between Congo and Angola. It then travels 1,700 miles (2,736 km) to where it flows into the Indian Ocean in Mozambique.

The Zambezi River winds its way through the wilderness in Zambia.

LAND OF LAKES AND RIVERS

In the far north of Zambia, the Rift Valley contains Lake Tanganyika, more than 420 miles (676 km) long and averaging about 31 miles (50 km) wide. Only a small part of the lake lies in Zambia. The lake area is a place of indescribable beauty, attracting visitors from around the world.

Zambia is named for the Zambezi, which means "Great River" in the Tonga dialect. For the first one-third of its journey, the Zambezi flows across a wide plain that floods at the end of the rainy season. Farther downstream, the Kariba Dam blocks the river's gorge to form the human-made Lake Kariba. Here, two hydropower stations supply electricity to Zambia and Zimbabwe. The Kafue River, likewise dammed for electricity, and then the Luangwa join the Zambezi before flowing into Mozambique. In northern Zambia, the largest river is the Chambeshi. It rises near the Tanzania border, flows into Lake Bangweulu and its surrounding wetlands, and emerges with a new name,

Victoria Falls on the Zambezi River marks the border between Zambia and Zimbabwe. Although there are various ways to measure the size of waterfalls—height, width, volume of water—Victoria Falls is usually considered the largest waterfall in the world. It is neither the highest nor the widest waterfall, but achieves that designation based on its combination of the two dimensions.

The United Nations Educational, Scientific and Cultural Organization (UNESCO), which recognizes the landmark as a World Heritage Site, calls it the "world's greatest sheet of falling water." It is more than a mile wide—5,604 feet (1708 meters)—and 354 ft (108 m) high. That's about twice the height of Niagara Falls, which is on the border between Canada and the United States, and more than twice the width of Niagara's widest section, the Horseshoe Falls. The falls are formed as the Zambezi cascades into a zigzagging series of deep gorges.

In 1855, the Scottish explorer David Livingstone was the first European to see the falls and named them after Britain's Queen Victoria. Of course, the falls already had a name, Mosi-oa-Tunya, which, in the Tonga dialect, means, "the smoke that thunders." The "smoke" in this case refers to the iridescent mist rising off the splashing waters, which can be seen from more than 12 miles (20 km) away. In praise of this astonishing natural phenomenon, Livingstone wrote, "No one can imagine the beauty of the view from anything witnessed in England. It had never been seen before by European eyes; but scenes so lovely must have been gazed upon by angels in their flight."

Today, the waterfall is known by both names and the official UNESCO designation uses both. The national park on the Zambia side is called Mosi-oa-Tunya National Park, and on the other side of the river, in Zimbabwe, a "sister" park is the Victoria Falls National Park. The spray from the falls creates its own ecosystem, sustaining a rainforest with plants that are otherwise rare for the region.

Kalambo Falls is one of the many spectacular waterfalls in Zambia.

Luapula. It feeds into Lake Mweru, emerges renamed Lualaba, which downstream becomes the Congo, and flows into the Atlantic Ocean. North-flowing rivers in Zambia flow to the Atlantic and south-flowing rivers into the Indian Ocean.

There are beautiful waterfalls on all the northern rivers. The most spectacular of these is Kalambo Falls, the second highest waterfall in Africa, which plunges in a single drop of about 726 feet (221 m) over the Lake Tanganyika escarpment. Many of Zambia's waterfalls have been declared national monuments, which means that they and the environment around them are protected from human damage. In traditional religion, the waterfalls were believed to be the abode of the spirits of the ancestors, but this has not prevented some of them from being used to generate electricity.

CLIMATE

All the rivers mentioned have their origins on Zambian soil, which indicates good rainfall. The country does in fact enjoy a favorable rainfall pattern, though there have been disastrous droughts.

A severe drought in 2016, the worst to hit Africa in decades, was exacerbated by climate change and an El Niño weather pattern. As a result of erratic weather—including late rains at the start of the season, drought in many areas of the country, and heavy flooding in other parts—farmers had lower harvests of maize, wheat, and sugarcane. This in turn, pushed up prices for Zambia's staple foods. For example, a 55-pound (25 kg) bag of mealie-meal (cornmeal), the country's ground maize staple, which usually costs about $5, was selling for as much as $12 in some parts of the country.

The rainy season, the equivalent of the Asian monsoon, traditionally starts around the end of October and lasts until March or April. The rest of the year can be totally dry, with clear blue skies day after day. Rain is, of course, vital for agriculture but has an extra significance for Zambia, where more than 90 percent of all electricity is produced by hydropower. The drought of 2016 left the water level in the Kariba and Kafue dams so low that it was hardly a few inches above the intake of the generators.

Zambia lies between 8 degrees and 18 degrees south of the equator and is therefore a tropical land. But the elevation of the plateau above sea level gives the country a more pleasant climate than that of most other tropical lands. The temperature on the plateau rarely rises above 95° Fahrenheit (35° Celsius). During the short winter, from June to August, there can even be frost on the plateau. The deep valleys, however, are much warmer, with temperatures exceeding 105°F (41°C). The hottest and most unpleasant phase is the period of six weeks or so before the onset of the rains, when people can get very uncomfortable. The first thunderstorms bring relief and refreshment.

The curving Kariba Dam on the Zambezi River stretches from Zambia on one side to Zimbabwe on the other.

VEGETATION

Most of Zambia is flat and covered by savanna woodland, open forest that varies in height and density according to rainfall and soil conditions. In the drier low-lying valleys the tree cover is much more open. Palms and enormous, fantastic baobabs are common. Where the forest is crisscrossed by drainage lines the land is suitable for agriculture, while the open plains of the Kafue and Upper Zambezi Rivers provide excellent grazing for cattle.

Where the forest has been cleared for farming it is possible to clearly see the abundance and enormous size—sometimes as large as a cottage—of the "anthills" built by termites. The termitaria (nests of termites) carry their own unique vegetation and during the rainy season sprout edible mushrooms; one type of mushroom has a cap one yard (0.91 m) in diameter, making it the largest mushroom in the world.

Although in some areas trees have to be removed to make way for agriculture, industry, and human settlement, extensive areas have been set aside as forest reserves. In the national parks the natural vegetation, from the tallest trees to the smallest flowers, is as much protected as the wildlife.

ANIMAL LIFE

Zambia has a multitude of species living in their natural habitats. Nineteen national parks have been set aside to conserve different ecologies and their wildlife. For example, the Kasanka National Park, adjoining the Lake Bangweulu Swamp, is conserving two rare antelopes—the black lechwe and the shy sitatunga. The Lochinvar National Park in the south is the home of thousands of red lechwes—long-horned antelopes that have adapted to life on a floodplain—and more than four hundred species of birds, especially waterfowl such as pelicans, spoonbills, and the huge Goliath heron. Other notable birds along the waterways are the African fish eagle and the Marabou stork, which nests in the cliffs of Kalambo Falls. Migrants from the northern hemisphere visit during the rainy season and bring the number of bird species recorded in Zambia to around seven hundred.

Lechwe antelope run across the grassy Busanga Plains in Kafue National Park.

The incredibly varied fish life of Lake Tanganyika is conserved in the marine extension of the Nsumbu National Park. The lake contains around 450 identified species, many of which, having evolved in isolation, are unique to Zambia. These include hundreds of species of iridescent cichlids and two species of the sardinelike *kapenta* (kah-paint-ah), which have been successfully transplanted to Lake Kariba. The largest fish in the lake are the giant catfish (200 pounds/91 kilograms), the Nile perch (130 lbs/59 kg), and the Goliath tiger fish (50 lbs/23 kg).

Kafue National Park and Luangwa National Park abound in big game, with thousands of elephants, buffalo, and large antelopes such as sable, roan, eland, and kudu. Lions and leopards are common, too. In Luangwa, a unique species of giraffe is found. Unfortunately the black rhinoceros is extinct locally, slaughtered by poachers to satisfy the market demand for its horn in East Asia. Elephants, likewise, are under constant threat for their ivory.

Thornicroft's giraffe, also known as the Rhodesian giraffe, is a subspecies endemic to Zambia's Luangwa Valley.

THE CITIES

Unlike other African countries such as Ethiopia and Zimbabwe, Zambia does not have ancient cities, either standing or in ruins. Most Zambians were semi-nomadic, their rulers shifting the government base from place to place at frequent intervals.

The country's current urban centers were all built during the past century. Their architecture and street plans are Western in style, and until shortly before Zambia's independence they were segregated along racial lines. In the Copperbelt, the towns started as mining camps, each close to a copper-ore body. Kabwe, the capital of the Central Province, was built adjacent to the old Broken Hill lead and zinc mine. Ndola, with a population of about 455,200, and Kitwe, with 504,200, are the largest cities in the Copperbelt. Kabwe has about 221,000. They are busy industrial and commercial centers, with the Copperbelt consuming more than 75 percent of the electricity used in Zambia.

The city of Livingstone, built as a commercial center on high ground overlooking Victoria Falls, was established when the railway from South Africa crossed the Zambezi on the bridge just below the falls in 1904. The town became the capital of Northern Rhodesia in 1911. It takes its name from the Scottish explorer and missionary David Livingstone (1813–1873), who spent many years exploring the Zambezi River region of Africa and trying to convert people to Christianity.

In 1935 Lusaka replaced Livingstone as capital, but the latter remains a place of great historical interest, apart from being beside the falls. Zambia's national museum, the Livingstone Museum, and an open archaeological site, the Field Museum, which is next to the falls, show the development of Homo sapiens in the area from the early Stone Age to the present, spanning more than 250,000 years of human history.

The early colonial buildings of the town give a glimpse of the more recent past, while the Railway Museum holds a fine collection of locomotives and rolling stock from the age of steam. For these and other reasons, not least Victoria Falls, Livingstone is known as the Tourist Capital of Zambia.

LUSAKA

In the early years of the twentieth century, Lusaka started its existence as a railway siding, a section of railway track used to allow trains on the same tracks to pass one another. It was named after the local chief, a famous elephant hunter, and grew to be the commercial center for white farmers in the district.

In 1935, because of its central position in the territory, the British colonial government made Lusaka the capital of the country that was then known as

Northern Rhodesia. They developed it on the pattern of an English "garden city." Buildings including the State House, the High Court, and the Secretariat were erected at this time, followed by the impressive Anglican Cathedral.

After independence in 1964, the imposing National Assembly, with its copper roof; the University of Zambia; the International Airport terminal; and many more state and commercial buildings joined the skyline.

Lusaka was planned for two hundred thousand residents, but today it has a population exceeding 2.4 million, most of whom live in poor conditions. From its beginnings as a small outpost of the British Empire, the city has transformed itself into the hub of Zambia and of Central Africa, with highway, air, and rail links.

INTERNET LINKS

https://www.britannica.com/place/Zambia
Encyclopedia Britannica provides a good overview of Zambia's geography.

https://www.lonelyplanet.com/zambia
This travel site offers information and photos of Zambia's various sights and regions.

http://whc.unesco.org/en/list/509
This is the UNESCO listing for the Mosi-oa-Tunya/Victoria Falls World Heritage Site.

http://www.victoriafalls-guide.net/zambezi-river.html
The Zambezi River is the subject of this tourism site page.

http://www.zambianobserver.com/population-explosion-puts-lusaka-at-risk-this-is-why-we-need-a-new-capital-city
This 2017 article argues that Zambia needs a new capital city.

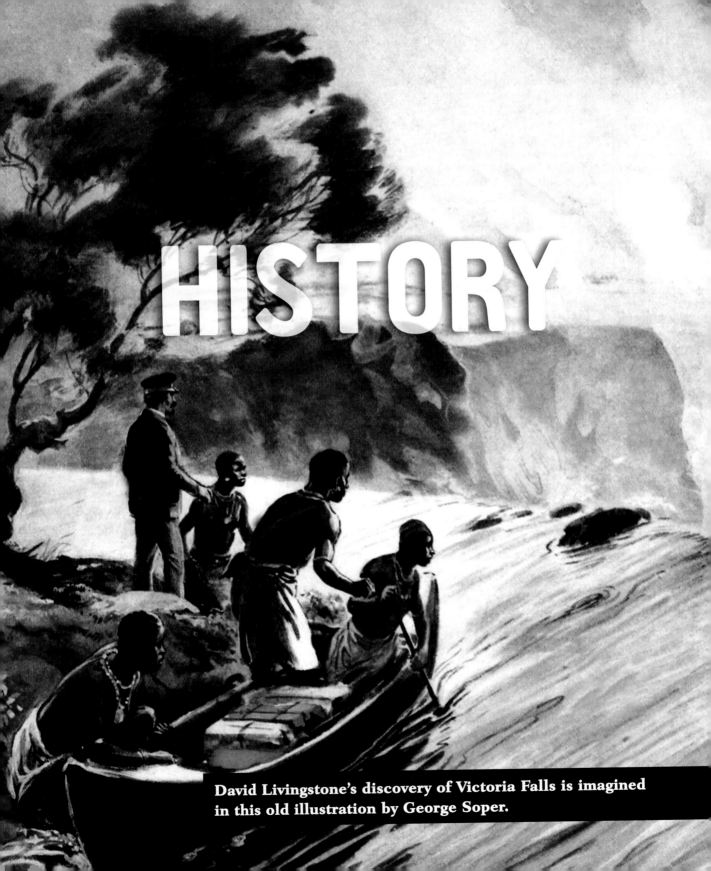

HISTORY

David Livingstone's discovery of Victoria Falls is imagined in this old illustration by George Soper.

ALTHOUGH ZAMBIA IS AN ANCIENT land, it is a relatively new country. European imperial powers created its boundaries on the map of Africa about a century ago, and it achieved its status as an independent nation even more recently. But humans and their pre-modern ancestors have lived there for a quarter of a million years, as archaeological evidence shows.

THE STONE AGE

About fifteen thousand years ago, during the late Stone Age, people evolved into modern humans, making sophisticated tools and decorating their rock shelters with pictures. These are the ancestors of the present-day San, or Bushmen, of southern Africa, a few of whom are still found in Zambia. They were of small stature and lived in family groups, following the herds of migratory antelopes they hunted. They also ate tubers, wild fruit, and honey gathered from the wild but did not grow crops, keep livestock, or construct dwellings. Skeletons found at one of their sites beside a hot spring in southern Zambia indicate that they suffered from tooth decay.

One of their hunting weapons was similar to the South American bola—stone spheres tied to the ends of a rope that when thrown

2

Zambia is the only country to start an Olympics as one country and finish it as another. In 1964, its athletes arrived in Tokyo for the Summer Games as Northern Rhodesians, and left as Zambians. The nation achieved full independence as Zambia on the same day as the Closing Ceremonies at the Olympics.

Zambia wants to bring Broken Hill Man home.

In 1921, a Swiss miner found an old skull deep in a lead and zinc mine in what today is Kabwe, a city in Zambia's Central Province. At the time, the place was called by

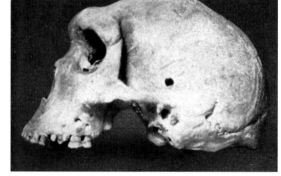

its colonial name, Broken Hill, Northern Rhodesia. The skull turned out to be very old indeed—that of pre-modern human of the Homo heidelbergensis *species (originally identified as* Homo Rhodesiansis*) who lived between 125,000 and 300,000 years ago. The fossil came to be called Broken Hill Man, or Kwabe 1.*

Aside from being Zambia's oldest human specimen, it also has the distinction of being the oldest known fossil to have tooth cavities—there are ten in the upper teeth. Scientists speculate that the poor fellow might have died of dental disease infection or a chronic ear infection.

His skull—the rest of his remains were never found—now resides in the British Museum in London. But the government of Zambia says the fossil is its own indigenous cultural property and wants it returned. The British government maintains that the skull was legally donated to the British Museum, where it is safely held for all of humanity; Britain has not, so far, shown any inclination to return it.

brought an antelope down by entangling its legs. These people are thought to have held the eland, the largest of African antelopes, as sacred; a surviving Zambian rock painting depicts the animal. The San lived in Zambia for thousands of years but were eventually superseded by the Bantu people who started arriving from the north more than 1,600 years ago.

IRON AGE IMMIGRANTS

About the fourth century CE, people who made and used iron, kept livestock, grew crops, and lived in houses began to occupy Zambia from the north.

They formed part of the slow migration of tall, dark-skinned people originating, it is believed, in the east of modern Nigeria. Over a period of more than a thousand years they took over nearly all of Africa south of latitude 5 degrees north. In parts of Zambia these people displaced the San; in other parts both lived side by side. The immigrants, known as the Bantu, were mining and smelting iron and copper 1,500 years ago and making weapons, fishhooks, and household items with the metals. They also baked clay pots and beakers. Around 1000 CE, further Bantu immigration gave rise to the ancestors of the present-day Zambian people.

Meanwhile, in what is today southern Congo, to the north of Zambia, two Bantu groups, the Lunda and the Luba, were developing into kingdoms. Between 1500 and 1750, offshoots from these kingdoms moved into Zambia. They conquered all but the southern part of the territory and formed kingdoms of their own. Previously Zambians had lived in small self-governing societies without a central political authority.

A young Bantu chief is portrayed in this 1878 illustration.

THE KINGDOMS

For a while some kingdoms in Zambia were ruled by the Lunda emperor, the *mwata yamvo*, but in time they all became self-governing. In the north were the Bemba, ruled by the *chitimukulu*, or chieftain; in the Luapula Valley, a breakaway Lunda tribe was ruled by the *mwata kazembe*; in the east were the Maravi, ancestors of today's Chewa; and in the west, on the Upper Zambezi, were the Lozi, who were ruled by a *litunga*. Each king made subjects of the surrounding inhabitants so that his nominal territory was extensive and held together by patronage and tribute.

In the first half of the nineteenth century, two new groups of conquerors arrived from what is now the Republic of South Africa. A host of Ngoni, led by Zwangendaba, and another of Makololo, who were led by Sebitwane, entered eastern and western Zambia respectively across the Zambezi. The Ngoni, who spoke Zulu, established a kingdom under Mpezeni I among the conquered Chewa.

The Makololo defeated and took over the Lozi kingdom. The Ngoni tried repeatedly to conquer the Bemba, without success, but secured their place permanently in eastern Zambia. The Makololo survived for only three decades. Weakened by malaria, to which they had no immunity, they were easily overthrown by the Lozi they had once subjected.

THE OUTSIDE WORLD MOVES IN

The first contact between different peoples is often the result of trade. From the earliest times in the Zambian area of the African interior, there had been exchanges of goods between producers of different commodities—for instance, between salt miners and metal workers or between fishermen and makers of cloth. Some of this trading, especially if it dealt with valuables such as copper and ivory, reached the coast.

The eastern seaboard of Africa had, from the days of ancient Egypt, been part of a trading network that extended to South and Southeast Asia and later to China. In the time of the Zambian kingdoms, this trade was in the hands of the Swahili, Muslim African-Arabs living in city-states along the coast and on nearby islands. By 1400 CE, people in Zambia on the Zambezi near Kariba were importing jewelry from Asia.

On the Atlantic coast, the Portuguese established trading ports in the sixteenth century. By 1850 their merchants had reached central Zambia. The Portuguese were also in Mozambique, having driven out the Swahili. They established a trading town on the Zambezi where it is joined by the Luangwa River. The Swahili of Zanzibar, too, were penetrating the interior, and by the mid-nineteenth century one of their merchants had crossed Africa from the Indian Ocean to the Atlantic.

Zambia thus became involved with both the Portuguese and the Swahili mercantile empires. Money was hardly used for trade. What the Zambian rulers wanted most were colorful patterned cloth, jewelry, firearms, and distilled alcohol such as rum and cane spirit. In exchange, they bartered local products such as beeswax, iron, copper, and the more valuable ivory, rhinoceros horns, and slaves.

From the west coast, the Portuguese shipped the slaves to mines and sugar plantations in Brazil. Slaves taken to the east coast could find themselves as far from home as the Middle East, India, and China. Many millions of Africans suffered this fate. Domestic slavery was an accepted part of the Zambian social order, and many kings took part in its natural extension, the slave trade, which was not suppressed until the end of the nineteenth century.

CHRISTIAN MISSIONARIES

Slavery was abolished in the British Empire during the 1830s, partly as a result of the moral crusade waged by Christian abolitionists such as William Wilberforce. One of his followers, a Scottish medical missionary named David Livingstone, started working in southern Africa in 1840. During a visit to King Sebitwane of the Makololo on the Zambezi in 1851, Livingstone saw the slave trade in operation and decided to help put an end to it. His plan was to establish settlements where slaves who were being exported would instead work at home and produce crops, particularly cotton, for sale in Britain.

Livingstone died in Zambia in 1863, without success in his venture, but his life and ideas inspired other missionaries. Two of the earliest of these were François Coillard, a French Protestant who opened a mission to the Lozi of the Upper Zambezi in 1884, and Henri Dupont, a French Catholic priest who did likewise among the Bemba in the north during the 1890s.

Livingstone was heralded as a great explorer in early illustrations such as this.

CECIL RHODES

The British born South African businessman, Cecil Rhodes (1853-1902), founded the De Beers diamond company in the country of Rhodesia (now Zimbawe).

Meanwhile, believing that Zambia was rich in gold, the British South African mining magnate and avowed imperialist Cecil John Rhodes was seeking ways to colonize the region.

COLONIAL RULE

From the 1890s until 1923, the area that is now Zambia was administered by Rhodes's British South Africa Company (BSAC) under a concession granted by Queen Victoria. Coillard had persuaded the Lozi litunga, Lewanika, to sign a treaty with the BSAC, and Dupont engineered the submission of the Bemba. Other kings—the *mpezeni* of the Ngoni and the *mwata kazembe* of the Luapula Lunda—were overcome by force of arms. Soon the whole territory was under BSAC control and the current boundaries largely drawn.

Rhodes's dream of Zambian gold did not materialize, but large tracts of land were taken over by white settlers. Although the BSAC abolished slavery, Zambians were subjected to a system of forced labor intended to supply manpower for the gold and diamond mines of South Africa. It was a new form of servitude. Direct British rule after the departure of the BSAC in 1923 was more benign, though the white settlers were highly privileged, and racial discrimination became the law of the land.

During the 1920s, the Europeans began to exploit the rich layers of ores deep underground along the Copperbelt. Skilled white miners were brought in from South Africa and Britain, while the large, unskilled workforce needed for mining was drawn from all corners of Zambia. From the Copperbelt, a Zambian national identity was forged out of the many groups that lived within the country's frontiers.

By the end of World War II, in which Zambian troops served with distinction in Burma, Zambia had become one of the world's top producers of refined copper. But Zambian workers in the mines suffered racial discrimination—the "color bar" that kept them in unskilled positions.

A trade union movement developed, and on the political front, the voice of Zambian nationalism demanded an end to colonial rule. Lawrence Katilungu headed the Mine Workers Union, while the nationalist leader was Harry Mwaanga Nkumbula, with his African National Congress (ANC) behind him.

FEDERATION

Another postwar development was the plan by the European settlers in Northern and Southern Rhodesia to consolidate their power by federating the two territories. Despite widespread opposition in Zambia, including by some whites, federation was imposed in 1953. The Federation of Rhodesia and Nyasaland, consisting of the territories of Northern and Southern Rhodesia and Nyasaland (present-day Malawi), was dominated by white supremacists and was a major obstacle to the establishment of independence for Zambia.

The Zambians' struggle against white supremacy and colonial rule gathered momentum. Nkumbula and his ANC seemed unequal to the task, and a new liberation movement, the United National Independence Party (UNIP, pronounced "yoo-neep"), was formed in 1958. Its most energetic figures were Kenneth David Kaunda and Simon Mwansa Kapwepwe.

So effective was UNIP's campaigning that the federation collapsed in 1963. Nyasaland became independent as Malawi a year later, in July 1964. Zambia became an independent republic on October 24, 1964, installing Kaunda as president. The British government retained Southern Rhodesia as a colony until 1980, when white minority domination gave way to majority rule and the country was named Zimbabwe.

INDEPENDENCE

Zambia entered independence with sails full of wind. Copper prices were high, and the economy was in good shape, promising the resources to correct the inequalities of the colonial past. Schools, colleges, and a university were built and health services greatly improved. Free universal primary schooling

Kenneth Kaunda, president of Zambia, in 1975.

was implemented, secondary school enrollment quadrupled, and adult illiteracy was tackled. Plans were drawn up to transform Zambia into a modern, industrialized state with the economy run by Zambians, not foreign-owned mining houses. It was anticipated that agriculture would outstrip copper as the principal earner of hard currency.

In November 1965, the dominant white population of Southern Rhodesia declared unilateral independence from Britain, and Zambia was drawn into what would become the Southern Rhodesian liberation war.

Apart from the material damage Zambia suffered, its plans for economic development were disrupted. In addition to the conflict between the black and white communities in Southern Rhodesia, Zambia was affected by the wars against the Portuguese colonialists in Mozambique and Angola, the struggle against apartheid in South Africa, and the war against South African occupation in Namibia. (Apartheid was South Africa's institutionalized policy of racial segregation and discrimination, which was in place from 1948 to 1994.) These events served only to distract the Zambian government from domestic priorities and to lead to the diversion of resources to unproductive expenditures.

By 1975 the Portuguese had withdrawn from Africa, and the Mozambique peace treaty was signed in Lusaka. But the war in what was to become Zimbabwe continued until 1980 and that in Namibia lasted until Namibia won independence in 1990. South Africa, meanwhile, was not freed from apartheid until 1994.

THE ONE-PARTY STATE

When President Kaunda introduced a one-party state in 1972, it was not, as many people had hoped, as a government of national unity in the face of the wars underway among Zambia's neighbors. Rather, it was a move to give supremacy to UNIP and to allow Kaunda to maintain his presidency by promoting unity and economic development.

Kaunda nationalized 80 percent of the economy, including the mining industry. The civil service, police, and defense forces were politicized, and an all-pervasive secret police force was created. Opponents were jailed, often for years without trial, with many tortured and some murdered. The president, who called his ideology Zambian Humanism, became a dictator. Though officially a "participatory democracy," the one-party state was authoritarian. Corruption, inefficiency, maladministration, and nepotism ruined the economy and perverted civil society.

The country was saved from collapse only when Kaunda was persuaded, partly by the donors upon whom the economy was by then dependent, to restore democracy. Apart from an abortive military coup in which no one was hurt, and sporadic rioting in which about twenty people were gunned down, no widespread violence occurred before Kaunda agreed to multiparty voting.

SUBSEQUENT ELECTIONS

Free elections were held in October 1991. Kaunda and his party, UNIP, were voted out of office by a wide margin. Former union leader Frederick Chiluba, who headed the Movement for Multiparty Democracy (MMD), succeeded Kaunda as president.

Zambian President Frederick Chiluba addresses the United Nations General Assembly at the UN headquarters in New York City in 2001.

The constitution of Zambia was subsequently amended in 1996, with Chiluba's government introducing a controversial provision that allowed only candidates whose families had been established in Zambia for at least two generations to run for presidency. This automatically disqualified Kaunda, whose parents were from Malawi. Presidents were also not to serve more than two terms in office under this new constitution. With these changes, Chiluba was elected to his second term as president in the November 1996 elections. In 2001 efforts by Chiluba's supporters to push for yet another amendment to the constitution, to provide for a third term of office for Chiluba, failed, and Levy Mwanawasa, a presidential candidate of the MMD, defeated all opposition candidates to succeed Chiluba as president in 2002.

Far from being a puppet of his predecessor, Mwanawasa began his term determined to fight corruption and spearhead intense efforts to reduce Zambia's foreign debt and increase economic growth. Huge economic challenges awaited the new president. In 2003 Chiluba was arrested and charged with corruption. The High Court in Britain ruled in 2007 that Chiluba and his aides had been involved in stealing a whopping $46 million from Zambia.

Zambian President Levy Mwanawasa addresses supporters during a rally in Lusaka in 2006.

In 2005, due to Mwanawasa's dedication to solving Zambia's economic woes, the World Bank approved a debt-relief package that wrote off more than half of the country's external debt. Substantial progress in privatization and signs of economic recovery began to take form with a series of budgetary reforms and the continued fight against the ravages of corruption.

PRESIDENTIAL DEATHS

In September 2006, Mwanawasa, respected for his integrity, was reelected to serve his second term as leader of Zambia. However, he died in 2008 after suffering a stroke. Former President Chiluba died in 2011. Michael Sata, founder of the Patriotic Front party (PF), and popularly known as "King Cobra" for his sharp-tongued fierceness, was elected the fifth president of Zambia in 2011. However, he died in 2014 at age seventy-seven of an undisclosed illness.

Edgar Lungu (b. 1956) of the PF became the country's sixth president in 2015. He was narrowly re-elected to a full five-year term in 2016, though his victory was challenged by his opponent Hakainde Hichilema. Lungu appointed Inonge Wina (b. 1941) as vice president, making her Zambia's first female vice president and the highest-ranking woman in the country's history. Born in Zambia, she attended high school and college in California before returning to her home country.

INTERNET LINKS

http://www.bbc.com/news/world-africa-14113084
BBC News offers an up-to-date timeline of Zambian history.

https://www.britannica.com/place/Zambia
Encyclopedia Britannica gives a good overview of Zambia's history.

https://www.nytimes.com/2014/10/30/world/africa/michael-sata-sharp-tongued-president-of-zambia-dies-at-77.html?mcubz=0
The *New York Times* obituary of President Michael Sata offers a look at Zambia's political history in recent years.

The Zambian coat of arms is full of symbolism, including the African fish eagle at the top, which represents freedom.

3

ZAMBIA IS A REPUBLIC WITH A presidential system of government, like that of France and the United States. The president is both the chief of state and the head of government. Unlike many African nations in the post-colonial era, Zambia has remained relatively stable, politically, and has been seen as comparatively successful democracy.

That's not to say the country has enjoyed smooth sailing over the last half century—not at all. It has endured several changes of constitution, authoritarian one-party rule, attempted coups, corruption, violence, and fractious elections. Nevertheless, it has so far avoided the civil wars, conflicts, and terrorism that have wrought tremendous destruction on some of its African neighbors, including Sudan, Somalia, South Sudan, Nigeria, Democratic Republic of Congo, and Central African Republic.

Suffrage in Zambia is universal, beginning at age eighteen. Citizenship is bestowed at birth if at least one parent is a citizen of Zambia.

In May 2017, the Zambian government announced a proposal to move the country's capital from Lusaka to the district of Ngabwe, where it would build a new city. Ngabwe is a rural area west of Kabwe in Central Province. Such a move is intended to decongest the severe overcrowding in Lusaka, which is unable to support its population.

THE CONSTITUTION–THEN AND NOW

Since independence in 1964, Zambia has had three constitutions. The current one dates from 1991, but has been amended several times, most recently in 2016.

The first constitution, negotiated at the time of independence by Zambia's nationalists and the colonial powers, was enacted by the British parliament. It provided for universal adult suffrage, a directly elected executive president, and a national assembly from whose members the president would appoint a cabinet. Freedom of association was enshrined, which meant that anyone could form a political party.

The first president was Kenneth Kaunda. His United National Independence Party (UNIP) had a majority in the Zambian parliament, with Harry Nkumbula's African National Congress (ANC) and a party representing mainly whites in opposition.

For a few years Zambia enjoyed a multiparty democracy, but UNIP had always been intent on a one-party state, following Kwame Nkrumah, the first president of Ghana and an influential figure in Africa's emancipation from colonialism. Kaunda appointed a constitutional-review commission, which toured the country to assess opinion and duly issued a report that broadly favored UNIP's plans. Kaunda, however, rejected its recommendation that a president should serve only two terms in office. After UNIP came to an agreement with Nkumbula on sharing the spoils of office, ANC ceased to exist, and the "one-party participatory democracy" was ushered in with Kaunda as president and a few ex-ANC members of parliament—but not Nkumbula—in the cabinet.

Under the constitution of the Second Republic, UNIP was the only party allowed. State and party were amalgamated, with the party supreme and the cabinet subordinate to UNIP's central committee. Parliament became a rubber stamp, and members who expressed criticism or asked awkward questions were removed. A state of emergency was permanently in force, so that citizens could enjoy only such rights as the president conceded. Radio, television, the press, and publishing were placed under state control.

By 1990 opposition to UNIP had become too widespread to suppress, and Kaunda reluctantly agreed to a new constitution negotiated with the recently formed Movement for Multiparty Democracy (MMD), which had the support of the Zambia Congress of Trade Unions. Civil liberties were restored, and the Third Republic was born, with Frederick Chiluba and the MMD winning the elections. The MMD had promised to review the constitution once again and appointed a commission, which included nominees of the opposition, to do so. The government accepted many of the commission's recommendations and presented these to parliament as amendments to the constitution. Parliament approved with a majority of more than two-thirds, but many people were unhappy that the matter had not been put to a referendum.

This third constitution contains a strong bill of rights similar to that of the United States and entrenches the independence of the judiciary. The president may serve only two five-year terms. But it contains two provisions that are contentious. One is its declaration of Zambia as a Christian nation. Many people, including some prominent Christians, would have preferred Zambia to be a secular state, with a clear separation between religion and

Much can be learned about a country—or its aspirations, at least—from reading the preamble, or introduction, to its constitution. Some countries barely bother with a constitutional preamble at all, while others introduce their constitution with lengthy, inspirational, and idealistic tracts. Preambles tend to spell out the principals and purposes of the government, verify its validity, and establish a national identity. Zambia's 2016 amended constitution begins as follows:

> *WE, THE PEOPLE OF ZAMBIA:*
>
> *ACKNOWLEDGE the supremacy of God Almighty;*
>
> *DECLARE the Republic a Christian Nation while upholding a person's right to freedom of conscience, belief or religion;*
>
> *UPHOLD the human rights and fundamental freedoms of every person;*
>
> *COMMIT ourselves to upholding the principles of democracy and good governance; RESOLVE to ensure that our values relating to family, morality, patriotism and justice are maintained and all functions of the State are performed in our common interest; CONFIRM the equal worth of women and men and their right to freely participate in, determine and build a sustainable political, legal, economic and social order;*
>
> *RECOGNISE AND UPHOLD the multi-ethnic, multi-racial, multi-religious and multi-cultural character of our Nation and our right to manage our affairs and resources sustainably in a devolved system of governance;*
>
> *RESOLVE that Zambia shall remain a unitary, multi-party and democratic sovereign State;*
>
> *RECOGNISE AND HONOUR the freedom fighters who fought for the independence of our Nation in order to achieve liberty, justice and unity for the people of Zambia;*
>
> *AND DIRECT that all State organs and State institutions abide by and respect our sovereign will;*
>
> *DO HEREBY SOLEMNLY ADOPT AND GIVE TO OURSELVES THIS CONSTITUTION.*

politics. The second is the clause stating that only Zambian citizens whose parents are or were citizens of Zambia may become president. First-generation citizens and those who cannot prove their parentage are thus unable to aspire to the highest office in the land. A large proportion of the population is affected by this clause. Among other changes, the amended constitution of 2016 rescinded a previous ban on dual citizenship.

THE EXECUTIVE BRANCH

The president is directly elected by an absolute majority vote in two rounds if necessary. The president chooses a vice president as a running mate, and selects cabinet appointees from among the members of the National Assembly. He or she serves a five-year term, and is eligible for one second term. Edgar Lungu was elected in 2015 to fill out the remainder of President Michael Sata's term, and again in 2016 to a full term. In 2016, Lungu of the Patriotic Front party (PF) won with 50.4 percent of the vote. His opponent,

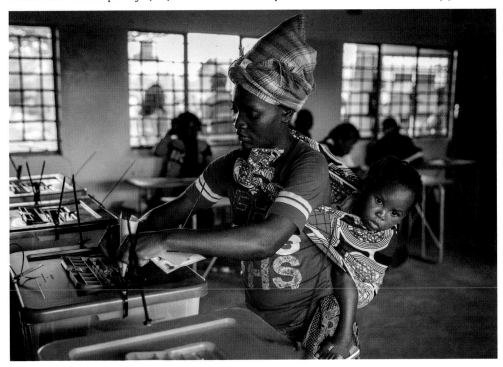

A woman casts her ballot at a polling station in Lusaka during the general election in 2016.

Hakainde Hichilema, of the United Party for National Development (UPND), won 47.6 percent. The next presidential election is to be held in 2021.

THE LEGISLATIVE BRANCH

Zambia has a unicameral, or one-house, parliament, the National Assembly. This legislature has 164 seats, of which 156 members are directly elected by a simple majority vote. Eight others are appointed by the president. Members serve five-year terms.

In the 2016 elections, the PF won eighty seats; UPND won fifty-eight; and the remaining eighteen seats went to independents or members of smaller political parties.

THE JUDICIAL BRANCH

The Supreme Court is the highest court; it consists of the chief justice and deputy chief justices, and at least eleven judges. A separate Constitutional Court was established in 2016, made up of the court president, vice-president, and eleven judges. Judges for these courts are appointed by the president, on the advice of a nine-member Judicial Service Commission headed by the chief justice. The nominees are then ratified by the National Assembly. Judges serve until they reach the age of sixty-five.

Lower courts include the Court of Appeal, the High Court, the Industrial Relations Court, Small Claims Court, and local courts.

INTERNATIONAL RELATIONS

Zambia is at peace with its neighbors and on friendly terms with all member states of the United Nations except Iraq and Iran.

The economy cannot sustain the cost of worldwide diplomatic representation, but Zambia has ambassadors at the UN and in some major world capitals. On its home continent, Zambia is represented in neighboring countries and in Kenya, Ethiopia, North Africa, and West Africa. It has established diplomatic relations worldwide with many other countries as well.

Zambia is an active member of the UN, the Commonwealth of Nations, and the Organization of African Unity.

On the economic front, it is a member of the Common Market for East and Southern Africa and the Southern African Development Conference. At both fronts the aim is to pursue regional cooperation. For decades Zambia, with the help of the UN and other agencies, has provided a safe haven for refugees from strife in Congo, Angola, Mozambique, South Africa, Namibia, Zimbabwe, and Rwanda. In 2017, Zambia harbored 25,063 refugees from the Democratic Republic of the Congo.

Zambian President Edgar Lungu addresses the UN General Assembly in New York in 2017.

DEFENSE AND SECURITY

Zambia has a small army and air force but has never been to war except indirectly. For example, the Zambian military played a defensive role when the country was attacked by Southern Rhodesian and South African forces during the liberation struggle against white rule in those countries. In the 1970s and 1980s, the Zambian government had allowed African nationalist fighters from those countries to use Zambia as a base.

Since then, Zambian troops have served with UN peacekeeping units in Rwanda, Angola, and Mozambique, but at home the defense forces are engaged largely in civil operations and are politically neutral. There is no conscription, though registration is required at age sixteen. Men and women ages eighteen to twenty-five may volunteer for military service as long as they are Zambian citizens and have graduated from high school. HIV testing is mandatory upon enlistment.

LOCAL GOVERNMENT

Zambia is divided into ten provinces, each with an administrative structure headed by a deputy minister appointed from parliament by the president. The country is further subdivided into 103 districts, each governed to a limited extent by elected councils responsible for such services as roads, water,

The constitution of Zambia guarantees freedom of expression and assembly, gives all citizens equal rights before the law, forbids ethnic and religious discrimination, and states that no person can be kept in custody for more than forty-eight hours before being brought before a court of law.

Despite that, its human rights record has not been stellar. A report released by the US State Department in 2017, for example, expresses concerns about serious human rights problems in Zambia, especially those pertaining to media freedom, police misconduct, and restrictions on freedom of assembly. The pro-democracy group Freedom House, rated Zambia's freedom of the press as "Not Free" in 2016.

In 2017, the international organization Human Rights Watch, reported that President Lungu appeared to be consolidating his power by suppressing dissent. In June 2017, he had his political rival Hakainde Hichilema arrested and charged with treason—a very serious charge—based on what was essentially a traffic violation. Hichilema's motorcade had failed to yield for the passage of the presidential motorcade. (Hichilema was released in August after the state dropped all charges.)

During his election campaign, Lungu, warned his political rivals and activists that "if they push me against the wall, I will sacrifice democracy for peace." Indeed, his increasing intolerance of political opposition prompted the Conference of Catholic Bishops to state that under Lungu, "Zambia eminently qualifies to be branded a dictatorship."

Whether that statement holds up over the remaining years of Lungu's term, and whether Lungu increases his crackdown on human rights will be determined in time. However, there is no question that Zambia has no tolerance for the rights of gay people and others in the LGBT community. In short, homosexual activity itself (never mind gay marriage) remains illegal. In 2013, shortly before becoming president, Lungu— then Zambia's Home Affairs Minister—made his position clear. "There will be no such discussion on gay rights. That issue is foreign to this country," he declared publically. "Those advocating gay rights should go to hell; that is not an issue we will tolerate."

health and hygiene, markets, and trading licenses. The councils, headed in the cities by an elected mayor and elsewhere by a chairperson, are supposed to finance themselves with revenue from licenses and rates. Very few are able to do so, however, so they rely on support from the central government.

CIVIC ORGANIZATIONS

Zambians take a great interest in politics. It is often referred to as the second national sport, after soccer, but the country also has many nonpolitical civic organizations.

During election periods, independent monitoring groups come to the fore, while several societies are engaged constantly in civic education and campaigns to promote awareness of civil rights and women's interests. Journalists have set up groups to protect and extend freedom of expression. Humanitarian organizations such as the Red Cross operate freely, while among businesspeople international clubs such as the Rotary Club and the Lions are popular and involved in charitable work. Chambers of Commerce and Industry, the National Farmers' Union, the Law Association, the Economics Association of Zambia, and other professional bodies comment regularly on the performance of the government.

INTERNET LINKS

https://www.cia.gov/library/publications/the-world-factbook/geos/za.html
The CIA World Factbook maintains up-to-date information on Zambia's government.

http://www.parliament.gov.zm
This is the official site of Zambia's National Assembly.

https://zm.usembassy.gov/2016-u-s-country-report-human-rights-practices-zambia
This is the 2016 US Country Report on Human Rights Practices in Zambia.

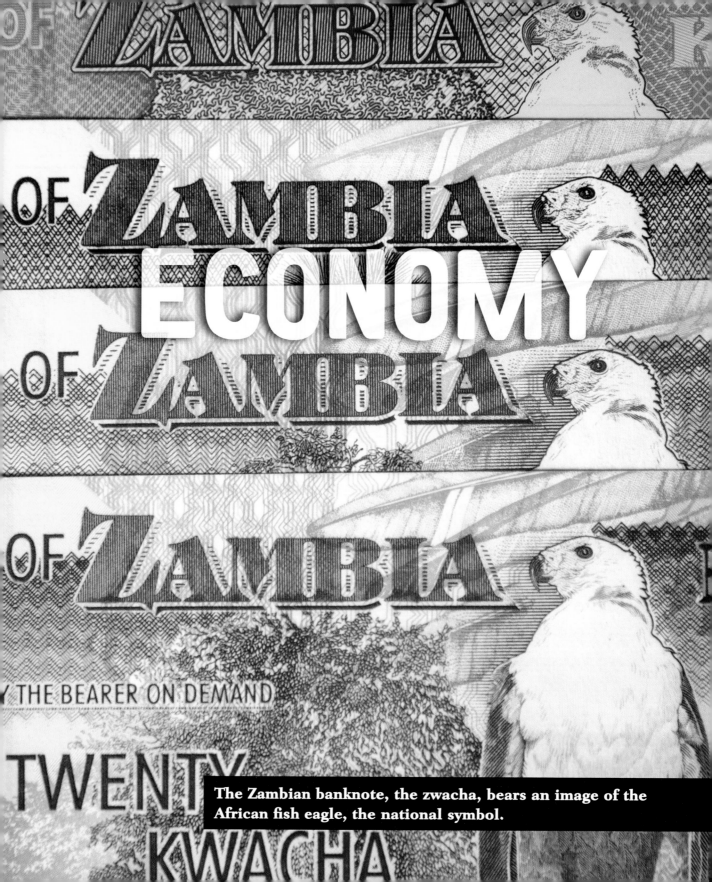

The Zambian banknote, the zwacha, bears an image of the African fish eagle, the national symbol.

4

THERE ARE MANY WAYS TO measure a nation's wealth—or lack of it. By almost any measure, Zambia is one of the poorer countries in the world, though it's not the most impoverished. About forty countries are even more destitute, based on most rankings. About 60 percent of the Zambian population lives below the World Bank poverty threshold. (The World Bank is an international partnership of five institutions that work to reduce poverty in developing countries. As a financial institution, it provides loans to developing countries.) In 2015, the international poverty line was determined to be $1.90/day.

Zambia lies on one of the world's great mineral belts, stretching from Congo in the north to the gold mines of South Africa.

Zambia had been doing quite well in recent years. In 2010, the president of the World Bank praised Zambia's efforts to reform its economy, noting that Zambia was one of the World Bank's top 10 global reformers that year. From 2004 to 2014, the country had one of the world's fastest growing economies, increasing about 6.7 percent a year.

A group of children sit in front of their mud shack home enjoying the early morning sun.

Although growth slowed to about 3 percent in 2015 and 2016, the economic outlook for 2017 is improving.

Despite that good news, however, Zambia has serious problems yet to overcome. Severe rural poverty remains widespread and there is high unemployment. The prosperity of the recent years has mainly benefitted the richer segments of the population in urban areas. Poverty in Zambia is largely a rural phenomenon, with 77 percent of the poorest households located in rural areas.

Social challenges, such as the heavy impact of HIV/AIDS, as well as the overcrowded cities and the high birth rate, continue to hinder the economy. Once a middle-income country, Zambia's average standard of living (as measured by GDP per capita) has fallen since it achieved independence, due to a variety of factors, including mismanagement, high level of debt, corruption, and the country's heavy reliance on the copper mining industry.

Zambia began to slide into poverty in the 1970s, when copper prices declined on world markets, causing an economic crisis in the nation. The

> ## WHAT IS GDP?

Gross domestic product (GDP) is a measure of a country's total production. The number reflects the total value of goods and services produced over a specific time period—typically one year. Economists use it to find out if a country's economy is growing or contracting. Growth is good, while a falling GDP means trouble. Dividing the GDP by the number of people in the country determines the GDP per capita. This number provides an indication of a country's average standard of living—the higher the better.

socialist government under President Kenneth Kaunda made up for falling revenue by increasing borrowing. When President Frederick Chiluba of the Movement for Multiparty Democracy party (MMD) took over in 1991, he found, in addition to the foreign debt, an empty treasury, a rapidly depreciating currency, and a soaring annual inflation rate. Much of the borrowed money had been spent on consumption, such as food subsidies, rather than on investment.

Copper provides 77 percent of Zambia's exports, and this heavy dependency on copper makes the country's economy vulnerable to fluctuations in the world commodities market—prices turned downward in 2015 due to a lower demand from China. Zambia also saw its status as Africa's largest copper producer usurped by the Democratic Republic of Congo.

MINING

Iron and copper have been mined in Zambia for close to two thousand years. Copper, smelted and cast into bars and crosses weighing up to 50 pounds (23 kg), was an important item of trade five centuries ago. Most of the existing copper mines in the country are on the sites of ancient surface workings.

The modern mining industry reached its peak in the early 1970s, when Zambia was among the world's top four producers of refined metal and the second greatest producer of cobalt, which occurs in some of the copper-ore bodies.

Today the mining industry's copper output is about half of what it was at its peak of around 771,000 tons (700,000 metric tons) in the late 1970s. This

A man works at a copper smelter at Mopani Mines in Mufulira, Zambia, in 2016.

is not due to a shortage of the ore but a result of the mismanagement the industry suffered during the years it was under state control. The industry is now privatized, and after a low of 251,000 tons (228,000 metric tons) in 1998, production recovered to 771,000 tons (700,000 metric tons) in 2016. Forecasts for 2017 and 2018 predicted production exceeding 1 million tons.

Copper and cobalt have long been among Zambia's prime metals, followed by lead, zinc, gold, and manganese. A large deposit of nickel awaits exploitation, and uranium, a small amount of which was once mined in the Copperbelt, can be found in several places throughout the country. There are also large deposits of iron ore, but it has not been economically viable to develop them. Mining is not restricted to metals. There are significant reserves of gems—in particular world-class emeralds, tourmalines, aquamarines, and amethysts. Coal is also mined, as are industrial minerals such as talc, marble, limestone, and glass sand.

ENERGY

Zambia has an abundance of potential energy resources, including rivers for hydropower, coal deposits, agricultural land to support the production of biofuels, enough wind for wind energy, and long, intense hours of annual sunlight to support solar energy generation.

However, wood remains the country's the major source of energy. Most households, particularly in rural area, use firewood and charcoal for their energy needs. Electricity, petroleum, and coal are mainly used in commerce and industry. This heavy reliance on wood has contributed to Zambia having one of the world's highest rates of deforestation.

Most of the country's electricity comes from hydropower. The major hydroelectric plants are at Kafue Gorge, Kariba North Bank, and Victoria Falls. There are smaller but economically important hydroelectric power stations in central Zambia, near Kabwe, at Victoria Falls, and in the north, one of which, near the Kundalila Falls, supplies the entire Eastern Province. Despite these plants, only 20 percent of Zambians have access to electricity, mainly because of their distance from the national energy grid. Even so, the nation grapples with electricity shortages.

Zambia has the capacity to export electricity to Zimbabwe, Botswana, Namibia, and South Africa. It is connected to the Congo power system, from which it imports electricity when drought affects domestic production.

Zambia does not have petroleum resources of its own, so petroleum products are imported from South Africa, France, and Russia. Crude oil is delivered by pipeline from the port at Dar es Salaam in Tanzania to the refinery at Ndola.

Efforts to develop alternative renewable energy sources have been minimal, mainly because of the high initial startup costs. Although the World Bank, USAID, and other nonprofit organizations are helping with energy development projects, Zambia's most pressing need is for increased international investment.

Flood gates are ceremonially opened at the Kariba Dam in 2015 after both Zimbabwe and Zambia signed deals with foreign investors to repair the massive structure.

AGRICULTURE

In agriculture, as in energy, Zambia has the potential to greatly improve its production. Maize, or corn, is the dominant crop. In 2017, the country was expecting a record harvest, up 25 percent over previous years, but that was during a season of above average rainfall. Agriculture in Zambia is still largely dependent on natural rainfall.

Agriculture is more than just another economic sector in Zambia—it's the way most people stay alive. Some 85 percent of the labor force work in agriculture, yet the sector contributes a mere 9.2 percent to the GDP. Only 14 percent of suitable agricultural land is currently under cultivation.

Most of the country's farmers are low-tech subsistence farmers. With better farming practices, such as crop rotation and the cultivation of soil-improving crops, Zambia has the potential to be an important exporter of grain. Climate and soils make large areas of the country suitable for crops such as sorghum, soybeans, rice, groundnuts, cotton, and tobacco. Wheat, coffee, and tea do well under irrigation during the long dry season. (It should be noted, however, that climate change is causing changes to the old, reliable weather patterns, and will no doubt influence the future of farming in this region.)

Farm workers load potatoes onto a truck for export.

Irrigation is the basis of Zambia's most successful large-scale agricultural enterprise, the Nakambala sugar estate, owned by the privatized Zambia Sugar Company. It meets the demand within the country and exports to countries such as those of the European Union and the United States. Other export crops, most of which are sold in Europe, are cotton, tobacco, and on a small scale, vegetables, flowers, paprika, and coffee.

Floriculture, the cultivation of flowers, is one of the fastest growing export industries. The production of roses accounts for 95 percent of the industry. In 2013, Zambia exported some $26 million worth of roses.

Cattle farming is of prime importance in regions free of the tsetse fly, which carries a deadly parasite. The fly is not common in the plateau areas of southern and eastern Zambia or on the Upper Zambezi Plains. Cattle have long been of great importance in the lives of the people there. Today commercial ranches are also large producers of beef, some of which is exported. Dairy farms, located mainly near urban centers, produce an adequate supply of fresh milk, which by law must be pasteurized before sale. There is a growing number of butter, cheese, and yogurt makers. Farmers also supply the cities but not necessarily the smaller provincial towns with chickens, eggs, pork, and fresh fruit and vegetables in abundance. But most farmers remain poor, and agriculture, particularly grain production, is not a success story.

MANUFACTURING

Manufactured goods—such as processed foods and beverages, chemical and pharmaceutical products, scrap metal, and textile and leather products—contribute about 25 percent to the country's total exports.

Government support of the Zambia Development Act, which gives generous investment incentives and tax breaks to industrialists—is helping to boost the manufacturing sector. With Zambia's resources of electricity, metals, minerals, timber, and agricultural produce (cotton, for example), the manufacturing sector has great potential for economic growth.

TRANSPORTATION

Landlocked Zambia has two operating rail links to the sea. Zambia Railways connects the country to ports in Mozambique and South Africa, while the Tanzania Zambia Railways Authority carries freight and passengers from Kapiri Mposi to Dar es Salaam.

International road transportation has become a booming business since South Africa came out of isolation with the end of apartheid. Much of its trade with central African countries passes through Zambia. In the 1970s, Zambia had one of the best highway networks in sub-Saharan Africa. Within twenty years, however, 80 percent of the road network had deteriorated. Today only one quarter, or 5,843 miles (9,403 km), of the country's roads are paved.

Zambian Airways was the nation's flag carrier, but it ceased operations in 2009. High fuel costs were given as the reason. This followed the demise of previous Zambian national carriers, leaving only Proflight Zambia as the country's only major airline. International flights are also handled by other airlines, including Ethiopian, KLM, Emirates, South African Airways, and Delta, among others. Main airports are at Lusaka, Ndola, and Livingstone. Altogether there are eight airports with paved runways, and eighty others.

TOURISM

In 2016, the number of tourist arrivals in Zambia numbered 956,782. This figure was a significant gain over the 859,088 visitors in 2012, and demonstrates growth in the country's tourism sector. However, given that the target since 2015 has been a million visitors, the number also indicates another year of falling short, if just barely. In 2017, Zambia's Minister of Tourism and Arts announced that Zambia was the ninth most popular tourist destination in sub-Saharan Africa. (For perspective, there are forty-six African countries that lie south of the Saharan Desert.)

Unlike South Africa and Mauritius with their beautiful coastlines and beaches, Zambia has not traditionally been a country for mass tourism. Tour operators to the country try to use that as a selling point, emphasizing its remote wilderness and lack of crowds. Topping the list of the nation's attractions are the awesome Victoria Falls and Mosi-oa-Tunya National Park. The South Luangwa National Park is famous for its walking tours during which visitors can have a close experience of wildlife. Lodges on the shore of Lake Tanganyika offer visitors the opportunity to bask in the beauty of the place and go fishing for the Nile perch and the Goliath tiger fish. Water sports from yachting to waterskiing are popular on Lake Kariba.

Following the journeys of David Livingstone and taking steam locomotive trips from the Railway Museum are among the many excursions that cater to the growing interest in historical tourism. Also of great interest are Zambian festivals, with their colorful music and dancing, which draw thousands of spectators every year.

INTERNET LINKS

https://www.fas.usda.gov/data/zambia-agricultural-economic-fact-sheet
The USDA site provides a fact sheet on Zambia's agricultural situation.

https://www.globallegalinsights.com/practice-areas/energy/global-legal-insights---energy-5th-ed./zambia
This site gives a good overview of Zambia's energy production and potential.

https://miningforzambia.com/copper-mining-in-five-easy-steps
This site explains the process of copper mining and features articles about Zambia's mining industry.

http://www.mota.gov.zm
This is the official site of Zambia's Ministry of Tourism and Arts.

ENVIRONMENT

A hippo enjoys bathing in a river in Zambia.

5

Z AMBIA FACES A NUMBER OF critical environmental concerns, particularly in the mining region of the Copperbelt. Air and water pollution, land degradation, deforestation, and wildlife depletion are all interconnected problems that can be blamed on human practices within the country itself. Climate change, on the other hand, is a looming threat that transcends anything Zambia alone is responsible for. Nevertheless, the country will need to adapt quickly to new and potentially more extreme weather systems.

POLLUTION IN COPPERBELT TOWNS

Acid rain—a form of air pollution caused by mineral extraction and refinery—has the ability to erode structures and injure crops and forests, as well as threaten life in freshwater lakes. Zambia is not spared these destructions. Copper mining is Zambia's economic lifeblood, but decades of copper, cobalt, zinc, and lead mining in the Copperbelt region has left thousands of children and adults at risk from lead poisoning.

Zambia has twenty national parks and thirty-four game management areas—with some 30 percent of its land reserved for wildlife. The oldest and largest is Kafue National Park, which encompasses about 8,649 sq. miles (22,400 sq km). Leopards, elephants, hippopotamuses, and cheetah are just some of the 158 mammals found there. Rhinoceros, which once lived in this park, were poached to extinction here by the 1980s.

A copper mine in Chingola is silhouetted by the setting sun.

In 2007, *Time* magazine named Kabwe, in the Copperbelt, one of the ten "World's Most Polluted Places." Financiers such as the World Bank and the Nordic Development Fund have supported Zambia's effort to clean up waste and resettle people after high lead content was found in blood samples, but the efforts so far have been small.

WATER POLLUTION

In the Copperbelt, mining has polluted not only the soil, making it incapable of growing crops, but also the rivers and streams. Leakages of copper sulfate, sulfuric acid, and other chemicals have turned waterways, including the Kafue River, into "rivers of acid" in the region.

In recent years, villagers in the area filed a lawsuit against Vedanta Resources Plc, the owner of Zambia's largest copper mines, the Konkola Copper Mines (KCM), alleging that the industry has poisoned their soil and drinking water. In 2015, after an eight-year-long legal battle, the Supreme

Court of Zambia ruled that KCM was guilty of "gross recklessness." London law firms have since filed for damages from Vedanta Resources on behalf of some three thousand people in the contaminated villages.

Other threats to Zambia's waters include runoff of nitrogenous fertilizer from farmlands. Victoria Falls—Zambia's only World Heritage Site—is under threat from river pollution as a result of tourism. The locals want resorts and lodges to be built near the falls and along the river banks to provide employment. Conserving the environment is not a huge concern. Environmental activists claim that the Zambezi River, which feeds Victoria Falls, no longer flows its natural course and has suffered a drop in its water level. As a result Victoria Falls is not as forceful as it should be. Overcrowded cruise boats add to the pollution.

Young women carry heavy bundles of firewood back to their village of Fwalu after gathering the wood several miles away.

DEFORESTATION AND WILDLIFE DEPLETION

In 2016, the Food and Agriculture Organization of the United Nations (FAO) reported that Zambia had one of the highest rates of deforestation in the world. Between 2000 and 2014, the country lost an average 682,063 acres (276,021 hectares) of forests per year to bush fires, agricultural encroachment, and mining. The illegal harvest of timber for use as firewood and charcoal adds greatly to the problem.

At a National Tree Planting ceremony in 2017, President Edgar Lungu said, "for us to promote forest conservation and reduce the pressure on forests as a source of wood energy, we must encourage the use of alternative domestic energy sources and sustainable charcoal production techniques."

Because forests regulate much of the catchment area of the Zambezi River, deforestation badly affects the water supply, especially during the

A baby elephant flaps its ears and trunk in South Luangwa National Park.

annual seven-month-long dry season. Efforts in protecting Zambia's land have been successful in some regions. This includes the national forest estate, which includes twenty national parks.

Zambia's wildlife suffers depletion from small-scale hunting for food by local people and from large commercial poaching operations, especially of antelopes, elephants, rhinoceros, and the large cat population.

CLIMATE CHANGE

Between 1960 and 2003, Zambia's average annual temperature rose by 2.34°F (1.3°C), and rainfall decreased by 2.3 percent each decade. That may not seem like much, but it is more than enough to make a significant difference in the nation's climate. And since climate change is still happening, it's hard to know where things are headed. Meanwhile, the rainy season has become shorter, marked by more frequent droughts. When rains fall, they do so with greater intensity and tend to cause floods. Over the coming decades, according to the Intergovernmental Panel on Climate Change, Africa is expected to warm up faster than the global average.

This is not a situation that Zambia, by itself, can rein in. The best it can do is plan for the changes ahead and figure out how to adjust to them. African leaders say they will need international help to build irrigation facilities, canals, and other climate-resilient infrastructure. And for Zambia, in particular, which is so reliant on hydroelectric power, decreased rainfall and more drought has decreased the volume of water in its rivers to the point where, at times, they cannot produce enough electricity. Therefore, the country needs to develop a variety of renewable energy sources.

Weather changes may also force farmers to adjust to growing different crops. This might mean shifting away from today's staple crops of maize and wheat, and planting drought-resistant traditional alternatives such as millet, sorghum, and cassava.

INTERNET LINKS

http://www.foilvedanta.org/articles/how-kcm-is-killing-the-zambian-copperbelt-part-1-water-pollution
This site provides in-depth coverage, with videos, of the pollution caused by mining in the Copperbelt region.

https://www.nytimes.com/2016/04/13/world/africa/zambia-drought-climate-change-economy.html
This article takes a look at the effect of climate change in Zambia.

https://www.theguardian.com/environment/2017/may/28/the-worlds-most-toxic-town-the-terrible-legacy-of-zambias-lead-mines
The extreme level of lead pollution in Kabwe is the focus of this article.

http://www.zambiatourism.com/destinations/national-parks
This travel site has information about Zambia's national parks.

ZAMBIANS

A young Zambian girl smiles against a pockmarked blue wall.

6

THE ZAMBIAN PEOPLE MAKE UP some seventy ethnicities, but most claim a common origin. North, south, east, and west, the legends of people who converse in different but related languages speak of an ancestral home in the ancient Lunda-Luba kingdom of the Mwata Yamvo ("ruler") in central Africa. They tell of a migration to what is today the Democratic Republic of Congo. Some people speak of origins even farther north, while the Ngoni and the Lozilay claim a South African heritage.

Apart from the more recent immigrants from Europe and Asia, Zambia is a broadly homogenous nation, with few of the ethnic contrasts that characterize Ethiopia and India, for example. Most Zambians regard themselves as members of the various tribes which had established their own homelands before European colonial powers redrew the map of Africa. Today, those Zambians consider themselves subjects of various traditional rulers, but still remain loyal to their nation.

In 2017, Zambia's population stood at about 16 to 17 million. However, the UN Population Division forecasts that Zambia's population will surge to between 100 million and 140 million by the year 2100.

ETHNIC GROUPS

Most Zambians are black Africans who speak Bantu languages. The colonial authorities, aided by missionaries, divided the inhabitants of Zambia into more than seventy ethnic groups. "Divide and rule" was a convenient policy for the imperial government, which maintained a strict control over the Zambian population through the chiefs it appointed and paid. Where a people did not have a chieftainship, the government created one. To this day a Zambian's reporting tribe and chief are recorded on his national registration card wherever possible.

The major groups in Zambia are loyal to the successors of the precolonial kings. Urban members of such groups travel long distances to attend

Zambia's population is estimated to be between sixteen to seventeen million people (depending on the source), with an annual growth rate of 2.9 percent. (Precise statistics are impossible to obtain, as births and deaths are not uniformly recorded in all parts of the country, and various organizations arrive at their estimates in different ways.) The population continues to grow because of the country's high fertility rate. This measurement is essentially the average number of children per woman of childbearing years. A rate of two children per woman is

considered the replacement rate for a population, resulting in relative stability in terms of total numbers. Rates above two children indicate populations growing in size, and the average median age trends younger, which is the case in Zambia.

In 2017, the nation's fertility rate was 5.63 children born per woman—one of the highest in the world. Although families in most countries can choose to have many children for any number of reasons, and provide for them accordingly, higher overall rates like Zambia's tend to indicate widespread poverty, among other factors. Impoverished parents with many children find it difficult to feed and educate their children, and it's also hard for women to be able to work outside the home.

What's the reason for such a high fertility rate in such a poor country? In Zambia's case, it's largely because girls and women lack access to education, family planning services, and employment. Poor, uneducated girls from rural areas are more likely to marry young. They will give birth early and continue having children. Women in poor Zambian villages view children as a sign of prestige.

They also know that some of their children might not live to adulthood. The infant mortality rate in 2016 was 62.9 deaths per 1,000 live births—a very high number compared to those of other countries. This means for each of 1,000 babies born in Zambia, about 63 will not live to see their first birthdays. (For comparison, in Cuba, which is also a poor country, the infant mortality rate the same year was 4.5 deaths per 1,000 births.)

traditional ceremonies, and chiefs often tour urban areas to stay in touch with their subjects. By merely looking at them, a person cannot classify the people into different groups as one can in India, where the Sikhs look distinctive from the Assamese. In fact the only distinguishable Zambians are the few unassimilated Batwa pygmies and San, or Bushmen.

CLANS

Besides tribal, or traditional, loyalty, Zambian people classify themselves by clan. Clans are said to have originated during the period of migration from the north. A party of migrants would name itself after a significant event, an animal, or a feature of the landscape. Clan names are sometimes used as modern surnames—for example, Ng'andu ("Crocodile"), Mvula ("Rain"), and Chulu ("Anthill"). All clan members, no matter what language they speak or how far apart they live, see themselves as belonging to one family whose members are expected to help each other. A Tonga "Elephant," for instance, is morally obliged to give help to a Kaonde "Elephant." Marriage between members of the same clan is regarded as incestuous and forbidden by custom. The clan system operates over much of Africa.

Clans that were once enemies have over the years transformed their aggression into a game called the joking relationship. This allows for ridiculing and mocking of the most extreme kind until everyone collapses in laughter. A joking relationship exists between the Bemba and the Ngoni, who in the past were often engaged in war. This tradition may explain why Zambians are generally great "talkers" but reluctant fighters.

A group of Batwa pygmy people live much the same hunter-gatherer lifestyle that their ancestors did.

What may be called Zambian royalty does not exercise direct political power. The constitution forbids traditional rulers from contesting in the election to the parliament or local councils unless they first resign their thrones. The constitutional House of Chiefs, whose members are selected by the traditional rulers, is given high status but is little more than an advisory body to which legislation is referred for comment.

However, kings and chiefs are revered by traditionalists as the intermediaries between their subjects and the spirits of their ancestors and, ultimately, God. In the traditional areas, which make up most of Zambia, it is the chief who allocates land and has the authority to withdraw the same. This gives the ruler great day-to-day power. Even under the 1995 Lands Act, a person in the traditional areas may obtain permanent title to land of his or her own only with the chief's consent.

Chieftainship is hereditary, but a chief may occupy his or her throne only after receiving recognition from the president. Apart from their subjects' tribute, chiefs receive a salary from the government, and their palaces are maintained at state expense.

These are some of the titles of the traditional rulers:

Tribe	Chief
Lozi	*the* litunga
Nyanja-Chewa	*the* undi
Ngoni	*the* mpezeni
Lunda	*the* mwata kazembe
Bemba	*the* chitimukulu
Luvale	*the* ndungu
Kaonde	*the* kapijimpanga

MINORITIES

There are three conspicuous ethnic minorities in Zambia. People with mixed racial heritage—African-Europeans and African-Asians—are one of them. They are citizens of the country but do not generally owe allegiance to a traditional ruler or belong to a clan. Among them are professionals and the business class, farmers, and skilled workers. During the colonial period they suffered racial discrimination and lived in segregated suburbs.

The second group consists of people who are confusingly referred to as Asians, whose forebears emigrated from India beginning in the 1920s, mainly as shopkeepers. Though a minority, they are a strong force in Zambia's business life, owning banks, real estate, and large trading houses as well as being prominent in other professions. Sometimes friction arises between the majority of Zambians and the Asians. Not all of the Asians are citizens of the republic, and the Kaunda government tried to force them out of the retail trade. But the relationship between this group and the majority is mutually beneficial.

Today there are probably about forty thousand white residents in Zambia. Many are temporary residents, employed via work permits in business, agriculture, industry, and mining. New legislation allows genuine investors to acquire resident status and to buy land, so the number of whites with a long-term stake in the country is increasing.

SOCIAL STRATIFICATION

In pre-colonial traditional communities the social structure was hierarchical. The Soli, people living to the east of Lusaka, provide a typical example.

According to Soli historians, there were three classes. The chieftainship was hereditary, with succession through the female line. Only a member of a specific clan, in this case the Beans clan, could become the chief. He or she had a council of advisors, often relatives, and their position was also hereditary. Below the councillors were the hereditary village headmen, who ruled the commoners on behalf of the chief. Chief, councillors, and headmen constituted the ruling class. The villages were usually family units made up of commoners, the middle class. At the bottom of the ladder were the domestic workers, who in the words of historians "provided free labor to the ruling class." These bonded workers were mainly prisoners of war or criminals, but the poor sometimes sold children they could not support into this class.

In modern urban Zambia there is no hereditary ruling class, though one of the reasons President Kenneth Kaunda lost popular support was the suspicion that he wanted to found a presidential dynasty.

Today's elite consists of those with wealth and political power, which enables a person to offer patronage and maintain a following. Except in traditional society, wealth and power count for more than birth.

At the bottom of the social scale are the unskilled workers and the unemployed. But this is not a rigid structure, and the extended family, which is Zambia's basic social unit, may contain members of all classes.

INTERNET LINKS

http://www.bbc.com/news/health-15433140
The BBC takes a look at "Zambia's Growing Population."

https://www.britannica.com/place/Zambia
This online encyclopedia has a good chapter about the people of Zambia.

http://www.everyculture.com/To-Z/Zambia.html
This site has a quick overview of Zambia's population.

https://www.theguardian.com/environment/2011/oct/24/population-growth-zambia-slums
This news article is a look at Zambia's population growth and urban poverty.

LIFESTYLE

A woman cares for her grandchildren, whose parents died of AIDS.

7

AMONG ZAMBIANS, FAMILY TIES ARE A powerful force, and the extended family is the keystone of the social structure. Broadly speaking, the extended family includes all kin related by blood, all of whom have obligations to each other— the richer helping the poorer, and the aged being cared for.

A man normally heads the family, but many Zambian groups are matrilineal—the authority and power to make decisions rests with the mother and her relatives. In traditional society this means that when a husband dies, his widow, children, and property are transferred to his mother's sister's eldest son. Today many urban Zambian husbands draft wills, entitling their property to their widows, thus sidestepping the system, but disputes are common, and widows often find themselves stripped of their inheritance by relatives of the dead man. Some Zambian men, including some Christians, are polygamous, and it is generally true that in any marriage the wife's position is considered subordinate.

BIRTH, CHILDHOOD, INITIATION

Zambia has a high birthrate, and half of the population is below the age of sixteen. In urban areas, expectant mothers can attend government prenatal clinics, give birth under medical supervision, and receive help and advice from postnatal clinics. Rural areas have fewer facilities, and some of these are provided by mission hospitals. It is not unusual for a

Zambian emigration is low compared to many other African countries. However, most of the people who do leave are the well-educated. Though the numbers are small, this exodus of skilled professionals has a major negative impact on Zambia. Zambia has few schools for training doctors, nurses, and other health care workers. Its spending on education is low compared to other sub-Saharan countries.

woman to have six or more children, though not all survive infancy. In traditional societies, children are treated as young adults as soon as they can perform tasks such as caring for younger siblings and helping about the house and in the fields. These days youngsters start school by the age of six, with many children starting earlier in the cities, where there are numerous preschools run by the government and private individuals.

In traditional families, girls and boys undergo an initiation ceremony on reaching puberty. Girls are taught about sex and the duties of marriage by older women. Depending on their ethnic groups, especially in the rural areas, boys are inducted into manhood by completing feats of endurance. After initiation, the "graduates" are considered ready for marriage. With the spread of Christianity and urban living, these practices are on the decline. However, many girls are pressured to marry at a very young age, which ruins their education prospects.

A young mother holds her infant in the village of Kawaza.

MARRIAGE

There are two types of marriage in Zambia. Statutory law covers marriages performed by a civic registrar or a licensed priest or pastor. Succession to the widow is provided for, and only the divorce court can dissolve the marriage. Traditional or customary marriage is a contract according to the laws of the community, and the traditional status of the wife and the community's rules of succession prevail. The marriage may be dissolved in a customary court. Both types of marriage are less a contract between two individuals than between two families; marriages are considered an enlargement of the extended family.

Another factor both types of marriage have in common is that the prospective husband is required to pay a bride price known as *lobola* (lorh-borh-lah) to his future wife's family. It represents not the purchase of the bride but a pledge and compensation for lost services; it must be returned if the marriage is dissolved. Traditionally *lobola* was paid in cattle or other livestock, but in urban Zambia payment in cash is common, and the parents of an educated woman may demand a high price. A high bride price may make it impossible for a man to marry the woman who has agreed to become his partner. The weddings of children from wealthy backgrounds are elaborate and expensive affairs.

A bridal couple poses with family members on the Luangwa River Bridge.

DEATH

When there is a death in a family, as many members as possible visit the home and family of the deceased. Every day at set hours, Zambian radio makes announcements of the recorded deaths, calling on relatives to come together. The deceased's family provides food and drink at the gathering, which may last for several days before the burial. Among Christians, a church service is conducted. After the funeral, the mourners gather at the house. In some traditional societies, the deceased's property is allocated after these rituals, and the relatives decide who is to care for the widow and her children. This tradition is especially beneficial for orphaned children whose parents have succumbed to HIV/AIDS. Migration to urban centers is breaking family ties. Extreme conditions of poverty are further eroding these traditional structures, and many orphans are being left with little or no support.

RURAL LIVING

Most land in the rural areas of Zambia is held under customary law. The chief remains the custodian of the land and the person who allocates it for use to his or her subjects. The people living in small villages are mostly farmers; some are traders, and some are government officials. Grain is grown during

Children sit outside a traditional house in a rural village near Lusaka.

the rainy season, and pigs, goats, chickens, and sometimes cattle are kept. Cotton and groundnuts are common cash crops, while fishing is an important activity near rivers and lakes.

Many villagers are farmers who live at the subsistence level, producing enough food for themselves and perhaps having just a small surplus for sale. Nonetheless they grow 70 percent of Zambia's grain. Poverty characterizes the social scenario in the rural areas. The Kaunda government attempted to improve matters by setting up collective and state farms, but these were a failure. Now laws allow the residents in the chiefs' areas to obtain personal ownership of land, a move the current government hopes will enable farmers to get credit more easily so that they can produce more and become more prosperous.

A typical village consists of thatched brick or lath-and-plaster dwellings, with a meeting place, the *bwalo* (bwah-lorh), at the center. Facilities such as schools and health centers may be a long distance away, and the roads are usually poor. During the rainy season some areas can be accessed only by helicopter, and following a season of drought, famine can become a dreaded reality in some places.

By contrast, the commercial farmlands held under private ownership mainly along the railway lines have a much more prosperous air about them. These areas occupy about 5 percent of Zambia's land and are farmed largely by the white farmers, who use modern technology such as irrigation and up-to-date machinery. With irrigation, two or even three crops can be harvested in one year. These farmers enjoy a comfortable if not luxurious lifestyle, and their workers, though often poorly paid, are generally better off than the hoe and ox-plough cultivators of the more remote rural areas.

Irrigation equipment showers a field of crops in Lusaka.

URBAN LIVING

The cities of Zambia cannot cope with the number of people who inhabit them. While vast tracts of the countryside appear empty of people, the urban areas, where some 40.9 percent of the population live, are overcrowded and noisy.

While a great difference in wealth does not exist among rural villagers, the cities exhibit the extremes—from the Hollywood-style mansions of the very rich to the squalid mud-and-plastic structures of shantytown dwellers. Between these extremes, the majority of urban residents live in small houses in the townships (as the poorer suburbs are called), in apartment blocks, or in dwellings they have built themselves in designated places provided with basic services such as water and sewers.

Statisticians talk of high- and low-density areas, a euphemism for poor and rich, and it is only the latter who are adequately serviced by the city councils. Residents of some high-density areas within easy walking distance of a city center rely on pit latrines, draw water from polluted wells, and suffer outbreaks of dysentery and even cholera. The Water and Sanitation

Late afternoon light shines across Lusaka and its suburbs.

Association of Zambia (WASAZA) estimates that only 65 percent of the population have access to safe water, mostly in urban areas.

The more prosperous areas, even if the roads are potholed, offer much that is available in developed countries—restaurants, five-star hotels, sparkling supermarkets, video shops. A satellite dish adorns many a suburban garden, along with a swimming pool and a tennis court.

But the cities, uncomfortable and filthy as they may be for the poor, are seen as places of opportunity. The drift into them will continue until the government implements policies that bring prosperity to the rural areas. Zambia faces an enormous challenge not only to lure people back to the country to cultivate the land but also to ensure that city dwellers are provided with profitable employment.

WOMEN

Men have traditionally dominated Zambia. The presence of female chiefs and the matriarchal system of succession did little to change the basic division of labor by which women were tied to the household and the fields. A woman's life was dedicated to bearing and rearing children and producing and preparing food. Men did not have to endure this routine. They hunted, fought off enemies, and mined and smelted metals when necessary.

As in many other cultures, in Zambia it is generally accepted that a wife must obey her husband. This is both a traditional and a religious habit. The missionaries started schools for girls, the objective of which was to educate them in a less competitive environment than that of the boys. Today, however, the Ministry of Education insists that there is no gender discrimination in the school syllabus.

Far fewer women than men complete secondary education, but measures are being introduced to correct the imbalance. For example, the government reserves 25 percent of its university grants for women, the remainder being competed for by men and women alike. Education and urbanization are working together to inspire women to carve an identity and make their lives more worthwhile. Issues such as the laws of succession have not been resolved to women's satisfaction, but women may now open bank accounts and obtain credit without permission from a husband or a male guardian.

Today there are women in all spheres of life—judges, ambassadors, doctors, lawyers, businesspeople. In 2015, Inonge Wina (b. 1941), a member of Zambia's parliament since 2001, became the first female vice president.

Zambia's Vice President Inonge Wina addresses delegates at the India-Africa Summit in New Delhi in 2015.

In the later decades of the twentieth century, a previously unknown virus began infecting people and puzzling doctors and researchers. By the 1980s, it had developed into a deadly epidemic worldwide. That virus came to be known as human immunodeficiency virus (HIV); *the set of symptoms and illnesses it causes is called* acquired immunodeficiency syndrome (AIDS). *The virus causes the progressive failure of body's immune system—its built-in mechanism for fighting disease.*

As the immune system stops functioning, the body is left vulnerable to life-threatening infections and cancers. Without medication, a person infected with HIV will probably die within nine to eleven years. The virus is spread from one person to another through blood, breast milk, and bodily fluids associated with sexual activities. Pregnant women can pass the virus to their unborn babies.

Researchers now generally agree that the virus originated in Africa, and though it spread throughout the world, the continent was particularly hard hit, especially sub-Saharan Africa. The devastating epidemic did not spare Zambia, which is still reeling from its effects today.

At first, many African leaders were unwilling to acknowledge the public health crisis because of shame, stigma, and the fear of discouraging tourism and business. In 1987, Zambia's President Kenneth Kaunda shocked the world when he publicly announced that his son, Masuzyo, had died of AIDS. Still, many African leaders continued to look the other way and international help was slow in coming. The plague devoured Africa. In 1993, out of about 14 million cases worldwide, an estimated 9 million of those were sub-Saharan Africans.

In 2000, some 15 percent of Zambia's population was infected, of which 60 percent were women. As AIDS victims died, their children were left orphaned—about 600,000 of them in Zambia alone.

In Zambia, as in many countries of sub-Saharan Africa, AIDS erased decades of progress in extending life expectancy. By 2001, the country's average life expectancy had fallen to an all-time low of thirty years! The virus also affected Zambia's economic and educational progress by killing large numbers of people in their most economically productive years—between the ages of twenty and forty-nine years.

There is still no cure for HIV/AIDS, but antiretroviral medications now exist that can extend the lives of infected people. In 2005, the Zambian government made the medications available free of charge for all who need them.

Although the crisis in Zambia is slowly abating, the disease is by no means beat. In 2016, 1.2 million Zambians were living with HIV/AIDS, including 85,000 children (birth–fourteen years). There were 21,000 AIDS-related deaths, and 380,000 children were orphaned by AIDS. In 2015, 4,700 children became newly infected with HIV—a dreadful statistic, to be sure, but a significant decline from the 13,000 new infections among children in 2010.

One of the biggest hurdles in conquering HIV/AIDS in Zambia is the public's general lack of education about it. Recent data shows that just 39 percent of the people have a comprehensive understanding of HIV, despite 90 percent having heard of the virus. Misconceptions abound. One of the most destructive is the "virgin AIDS cure myth"—the widespread belief that infected men can be cured by having intercourse with sexually inexperienced young girls. Not only does this behavior not cure the man, it spreads the disease to the girl, who was often an unwilling participant to begin with.

Children greet their volunteer teacher at the Ipusukilo Community School, where many of the students are HIV/AIDS orphans.

EDUCATION

At the time of independence there were only 120 Zambians with university degrees and a mere one thousand who had completed secondary education. It was around this same time that the mining companies started to recruit Zambians for skilled work.

One of President Kenneth Kaunda's primary goals was the rapid growth and expansion of educational opportunities. Within a few years of independence, secondary schools were built in all seventy-two districts of the country. Universal free primary education was introduced, and at the other end of the ladder, the University of Zambia was opened in Lusaka. Technical colleges were expanded or established from scratch, and the University Teaching Hospital was built in Lusaka to train physicians. The Natural Resources Development College set about training students for careers in agriculture, among other disciplines, and the National Institute for Public Administration prepared students for the civil service. Later the Copperbelt University, dealing with technical subjects, opened at Kitwe. However, the government could not keep up the initial momentum in this field. By the 1980s, much of the education system was in decay. In 1997 only 16 percent of secondary-school graduates who qualified for university could be accommodated.

The post-1991 government established a program to rehabilitate schools, many of which had no desks or even windowpanes. The responsibility of school management was passed from the Ministry of Education to school boards on which parents are represented.

Statistics—some of which differ greatly by source—show that in 2015, almost all children of both genders were enrolled in elementary school (grades 1—7), which is free, but that many dropped out before reaching grade 7. Enrollment in basic (grades 8—9) and secondary school (10—12) was much lower, only about one third of the children. Some remote areas don't even have secondary schools. Above 7th grade, education is no longer free. The government spends very little on education, about 1.1 percent of GDP, which is almost the lowest of any country on earth. Primary school teachers are very minimally paid, or are volunteers. Educational standards for both teachers and students are very low.

The University of Zambia, located in Lusaka and established in 1965, is the country's oldest university. It accommodates about fifteen- to twenty thousand students, both Zambian and international, in a variety of undergraduate and graduate programs. Copperbelt University in Kitwe was established in 1987 and serves about ten- to fifteen thousand students. Among its programs are medical studies, mines and mineral sciences, mathematics and natural sciences, natural resources, engineering, and business.

INTERNET LINKS

https://www.avert.org/professionals/hiv-around-world/sub-saharan-africa/zambia
This site offers up-to-date information about HIV and AIDS in Zambia.

https://www.lusakatimes.com/2015/01/26/inonge-winas-full-profile
A profile of Inonge Wina, the country's first woman vice president, is provided on this site.

https://www.unicef.org/infobycountry/zambia_statistics.html
UNICEF has extensive statistics relating to health, education, and other lifestyle issues of Zambia's women and children.

https://www.unicef.org/zambia/education_18701.html
UNICEF highlights its education-related initiatives in Zambia.

RELIGION

People attend a service at the Chipembi United Church in Lusaka.

8

CHRISTIANITY MADE A DEEP IMPACT on the development of Zambia, as it was the missionaries who introduced Western education. They were also in the forefront of the movement to suppress the slave trade in the nineteenth century, some of the first mission stations being refuges for liberated slaves. But thereafter missionaries worked hand in hand with the colonial government. Nearly all the leaders of the struggle for independence came out of mission schools.

TRADITIONAL RELIGION

When missionaries started work in what is now Zambia, they found that the people there already had their own beliefs. Although it had no written texts, the traditional religion of Bantu-speaking people, who made up much of Africa's population, was and still is a coherent system of belief. The supreme god, who is known as *Lesa*, among other names, is the creator of the world and everything in it. Mankind was created immortal and only later became subject to death, but human spirits live on, intervening in human affairs and in relations with Lesa. The spirits are, therefore, honored and even worshiped.

The preamble to the current constitution declares Zambia to be a Christian nation but does not make Christianity the state religion. Freedom of religion is guaranteed. However, in 2016, President Edgar Lungu created a new Ministry of National Guidance and Religious Affairs, a controversial move that many fear will lead to government meddling in the churches.

Pastor Chibwe Katebe sings exultantly during a service at the House of Prayer for All Nations in Livingstone.

The living and the dead form part of a single community, joined together through certain individuals, notably the chiefs, who are also looked upon as priests in some sense, and through mediums, who are believed to be possessed by the spirits. The spirits can be either benign or evil, the latter being the power behind what Westerners call witchcraft, which brings disease, misfortune, and death.

The land remains the foundation of human life in this community. Thus a chief's authority in allocating land has a spiritual as well as a political significance.

Because it is believed that a person's spirit lives on, there is no belief in reincarnation, nor is there a belief in punishment (hell) or reward (heaven) for behavior in the afterlife. People enjoy or suffer their just desserts while on earth, and there is no notion of personal redemption or salvation. Lesa, as supreme god, is present but does not direct human affairs as the Jewish and Christian Jehovah is believed to. In times of trouble or to ward off bad times, people will try to appease the spirits with offerings and sacrifices.

CHRISTIANITY

About 95.5 percent of Zambians are Christian, with some 75.3 percent being Protestants and 20.2 percent being Roman Catholics. However, a portion of those, around 11 percent, may also practice traditional indigenous religions. The earliest missionaries in Zambia were Protestants of the reformed churches, represented by the Paris Evangelical Missionary Society and the London Missionary Society, to which David Livingstone, the antecedent of all the missionaries, had belonged. Most of the reformed churches are now amalgamated in the United Church of Zambia. Other established denominations are Anglican, Pentecostal, Presbyterian, Lutheran, Baptist, Seventh-Day Adventist, Jehovah's Witness, and a variety of evangelical denominations. There are also a growing number of charismatic fundamentalist groups that take the Bible as literal truth. Eastern Christianity is represented by the Greek and Coptic Orthodox churches.

Cathedral of the Holy Cross is an Anglican church in Lusaka.

There are also some Africanist sects, which fuse Christianity with traditional religion. Today the most visible Africanist church is that of the Zion Apostolics, whose bearded leaders, or prophets, take many wives, like King Solomon of old. A self-sufficient group originating in the suburb of Korsten, outside Port Elizabeth, South Africa, members were at first basket makers but are now also proficient tinkers and metalworkers and work on communal farms. One of Lusaka's suburbs, *Mandevu*, which means "Bearded," is named after them. The church has branches all over central and southern Africa.

Of the mainstream churches, the Roman Catholic has gone furthest in Africanizing itself. Colorful ceremonies with drumming, singing, and dancing are part of its Zambian liturgy. This church in particular opposed the one-party state and was instrumental in its downfall, with the bishops openly condemning its corruption and dictatorial practices. But today many regard the Catholic Church's opposition to contraception as well as condoms as a precaution against HIV/AIDS, as reactionary and obstructive to solving some of Zambia's biggest problems.

The fundamentalist groups are influenced by the TV evangelism emanating from the United States. These groups hold crusades and demonstrations of faith healing and invite people to be "born again" in Jesus Christ. Their members are known colloquially as born again.

Although various churches disagree on many matters of doctrine and practice, they jointly produce a weekly Christian newspaper, *The National Mirror*, and sometimes work together on social projects. The larger denominations have schools, orphanages, and hospitals of their own, which render valuable services to the country as a whole.

ISLAM AND OTHER FAITHS

Islam was established in the city-states of the east African coast eight hundred years ago, having been introduced by the Arabs and, some believe, Iranian traders. In the second half of the nineteenth century, Zanzibar was the principal city of the coast, and merchants from there traveled into the interior of central Africa, taking Islam with them. No large Muslim communities developed in Zambia from this source, perhaps because Islamic Zanzibar was associated with the slave trade. However, in Malawi, Zambia's eastern neighbor, many people were converted. Muslims in Zambia are mainly immigrants from the Indian subcontinent and their descendants who have settled along the railroad line from Lusaka to Livingstone, in Chipata, and in the rest of Eastern Province.

Mosques are prominent in the main urban centers, and the Muslim community is well known for its charitable work, which includes assistance to Christian hospitals. The Islamic Foundation near Lusaka offers welfare facilities and schooling to young Zambians, and its activities may lead to an increasing number of converts. Islamic propagation societies are offering free education to impoverished rural populations. Many Christian families have sent their children to Muslim schools in the hope that an Islamic education is better than none.

Zambia's Asian community also includes many Hindus. Other faiths include the Sikhs, the Baha'i, and a small number of Buddhists and Jews.

The white Umar al-Farooq Mosque gleams against a blue sky.

INTERNET LINKS

https://www.christiantoday.com/article/christians.fear.state.control.of.religion.in.zambia/96078.htm
This 2016 article discusses concerns that Zambia's government might take control of religion.

https://www.daily-mail.co.zm/ministry-of-religion-to-entrench-christian-values/
This editorial opinion in the *Zambia Daily Mail* takes the opposite view of the issue discussed above.

https://www.state.gov/j/drl/rls/irf/2007/90127.htm
The US Department of State issued this report on religion in Zambia.

LANGUAGE

A boy carries a well-worn schoolbook written in English.

9

WALISHIMBA ICIBEMBA? ("DO YOU speak Bemba?) *Na wa bulela se Rotse?* ("Do you speak Lozi?) *Mumalankhula chinyanja?* ("Do you speak Nyanja?") No? Well, in that case, *Walishimba icisungu? Na wa bulela sikuwa? Mumalankhula chingelesi?* (All mean "Do you speak English?" in Bemba, Lozi, and Nyanja, in that order.)

What language is a country of more than seventy indigenous languages or dialects supposed to speak? As independence approached, Zambians engaged in a heated debate over the choice of an official language for the postcolonial state.

Pan-Africanists—those who favor a united Africa—favored Swahili, the main language of Tanzania, Kenya, Uganda, and the Comoro Islands. It is also spoken in parts of Congo, Mozambique, and Somalia, as well as in small areas in Zambia itself. Swahili had the advantage of being closely related to Zambian languages and of not being the tongue of any specific nation or group, having evolved along the African east coast in an interaction between local dialects and Arabic. The pan-Africanist view was that by adopting Swahili, Zambia would be taking an important step toward the goal of African unity and replacing English with a language untainted by colonialism.

Those favoring the retention of English argued that it was the most widely used international language. If it had been the tongue of foreign rule, that was now irrelevant. They added that Swahili had, in any case, been the language of Zanzibari slave traders, who had wreaked havoc in the country before the British put a stop to their activities.

As things turned out, English was chosen. Swahili as an alternative has been largely forgotten, to the extent that it is not even taught in schools or universities. The preferred second international language today is French.

OFFICIAL AND SEMIOFFICIAL LANGUAGES

As the official language, English is used in all government offices and by the police and the defense forces. The constitution and all legislation are written and published in English, and hearings in the high court and the magistrates' courts are conducted in English, with translation when necessary by interpreters. The business of the National Assembly is carried out in English, and candidates seeking election must by law show that they can use it

A road sign in Nyimba, Zambia, is written in the country's official language.

In Zambia, English has acquired some peculiarities. For example:

Butchery — Butcher's shop

Honda — Any motorcycle

Saladi — Any salad or cooking oil

Surf — Any washing powder

Vanette — Small pickup truck

Beer — Any alcoholic drink, as in, "Whisky is my favorite beer."

FOREIGN INFLUENCES

Zambian languages have absorbed and adapted words from outsiders. For example:

Bemba's citabu *(chi-tah-boo) is from* kitab, *Swahili/Arabic for "book."*

Nyanja's tirigo *(tee-ree-goh) is from* trigo, *Portuguese for "wheat."*

Nyanja's nsapato *(n-sah-pah-too) is from* sapato, *Portuguese for "shoe."*

Luvale's njanena *(n-jah-nair-nah) is from* janela, *Portuguese for "window."*

Nyanja's galimoto *(gah-lee-morh-torh) is from the English "motorcar."*

proficiently. English is almost the exclusive language of radio, television, and the press. It is the language of domestic and international business and also the country's *lingua franca*, enabling people with different mother tongues to communicate.

There are seven local languages that have semiofficial status: Bemba, Kaonde, Lozi, Lunda, Luvale, Nyanja, and Tonga. They are used in the local courts, which deal with litigation under customary or traditional law. They share one radio channel and have about an hour each on television every day.

Bemba, Kaonde, Lunda, Luvale, and Nyanja derived from the ancient Lunda-Luba empire. Tonga was brought by earlier arrivals from the north, while modern Lozi comes from the nineteenth century Sotho language of the Kololo invaders from the south. The other invaders from the south, the Ngoni, have lost their original Zulu tongue and now speak Nyanja.

ZAMBIAN PROVERBS

Proverbs express succinctly the ethical codes and social relations of the people from whom they spring. Many are relevant to daily behavior, and proverbs from the people as distant from each other as the English and the Bemba are sometimes startlingly similar. The following are from various Zambian groups:

Bemba

- *A child who does not travel praises his mother as the best cook.*
- *Those who eat iguanas are found close to each other.*

Kaonde

- *The mouth gets the head into trouble.*
- *If you followed what a chicken eats, would you eat the chicken?*

Lozi

- *One finger cannot crush a louse.*
- *A cow does not find its own horns heavy.*

Luvale

- *Firewood for cooking an elephant is gathered by the elephant itself.*
- *The snake bites because its hole is blocked.*

Nyanja

- *The person who does not listen learns when he is struck by an ax.*
- *If you are ugly, know how to dance.*

Tonga

- *He who asks won't be poisoned by mushrooms.*
- *Wisdom can come from even a small anthill.*
- *It takes more than one day for an elephant to rot.*

THE LANGUAGE FAMILY

The Zambian languages are members of the extensive family of Bantu languages spoken from southern Sudan in the north to South Africa and include tongues as widely used as Swahili, Lingala (in Congo), and Zulu.

The Bantu people are believed to have their roots in eastern Nigeria, and the languages are related to some of those in West Africa.

It is said in Zambia that a Lungu-speaking person from the shore of Lake Tanganyika who walks from village to village for 1,000 miles (1,609 km) to reach Victoria Falls will experience no difficulty with language, as one dialect merges into another along the length of the route. The hiker would cross the Chambeshi River shortly after starting the journey and would end the trip on the banks of the Zambezi. The names of both rivers mean the same, "Big Water": *Cha* and *za* both mean "big," and *mbeshi* and *mbezi* mean "water."

The way Bantu languages work is unique. The system is based on the root of the noun, and nouns fall into different classes, each bearing a prefix that is transferred to the verb and the adjective. To take two short examples: the root *ntu* (in-too) signifies "essence," and the prefix *mu* signifies "living." Thus *muntu* means "person" or "human being." The plural of *mu* is *ba*, so *bantu* means "people." The prefix *i* signifies "inanimate." Thus *intu* means "thing," and *izintu* means "things." A sentence is held together by the prefixes, for example:

Izintu	*zonse*	*zanga*	*zagwa.*
Things	all	mine	are falling down.

The Bantu languages are the most alliterative in the world.

WRITING

Missionaries, who used the Roman alphabet, were the first to put Zambian languages into writing. One of the earliest newspapers in Zambia, the French evangelicals' *Liseli* ("The Pleiades"), was published in Lozi in the early twentieth century. Major parts of the Bible have been translated into Zambian

A teacher instructs her students at a primary school near the Kafue National Park.

languages. In the 1950s, the government set up the African Literature Bureau to prepare and publish texts in Zambian languages, laying the basis for nonreligious literary works.

The seven African languages recognized by the government as national and given semiofficial status is in fact a compromise, as there are seventy or more Bantu languages in use, and some groups feel they have been left out. It is, however, difficult to draw the line between language and dialect, so it is likely the position will not be altered.

LANGUAGE AND EDUCATION

The first years of primary education are given in the semiofficial language predominant in the area: Bemba in Northern Province, for instance, and

Nyanja in Eastern Province and Lusaka. Disputes in the past over the boundaries of school language areas were settled by compromise. English is introduced in second grade, and in fifth grade, it becomes the sole language of instruction, with the Zambian languages studied as subjects. Where resources allow, French is introduced in secondary schools. English is the medium at the University of Zambia and the Copperbelt University. English dominates in Zambian intellectual discourse and has without doubt helped to unite the nation across its linguistic divides, as minor as they may be. On the other hand, many people say that Zambian languages must develop if they are to play their rightful role in the national culture.

INTERNET LINKS

http://www.dw.com/en/zambia-grapples-with-language-challenge/a-16598662
This article discusses the problem of language in Zambia.

https://www.omniglot.com/writing/bemba.php
Omniglot offers an introduction to the Bemba language, with links to many other African languages spoken in Zambia.

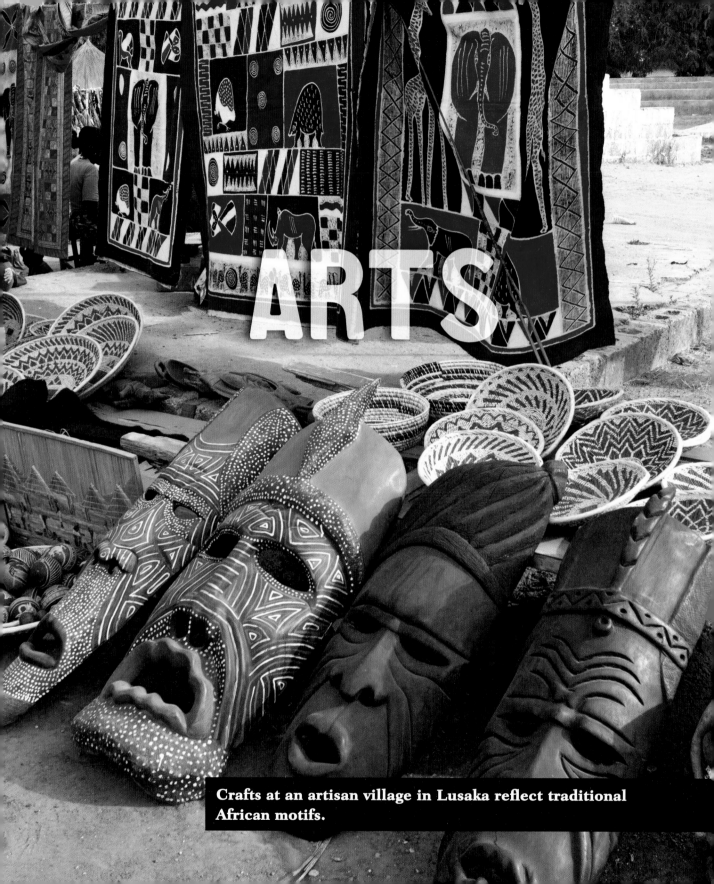

ARTS

Crafts at an artisan village in Lusaka reflect traditional African motifs.

10

ONE OF THE DESTRUCTIVE THINGS about colonialism, in general, is that the imperial power seeks to impose its culture—which it inevitably sees as superior—on its colonized subjects. Indigenous religions, languages, and customs are usually discouraged, or even forbidden. So it was with the European nations that colonized Africa in the nineteenth century.

The traditional arts of Zambia suffered severely during the colonial period. The crafts of the potter and the metalworker were driven almost to extinction by the import of factory-made goods. Music, song, and dance, being associated with rituals and ceremonials, were discouraged and in some instances forbidden by missionaries and the government. The missionaries saw them as manifestations of a pagan culture that should be replaced by Christian civilization. From the colonial government's standpoint, any form of artistic expression that mocked it or reminded people that they had once ruled themselves was a threat to its authority. These arts were trivialized, stripped of their spiritual context, and turned into tourist entertainment.

Similarly, the people's oral tradition—the poetry and stories that formed an unwritten scripture of traditional religion—was ignored by missionaries unless it could be fitted into the Christian pattern of belief.

In 1975, President Kenneth Kaunda decreed that 90 percent of radio airtime be devoted to Zambian music. Foreign artists were relegated to the remaining 10 percent. In the 1980s, the requirement was eased. Many musicians credit Kaunda with jumpstarting the Zambian music business and creating a domestic audience.

The Bible, as interpreted by the church, became the source of authority and truth.

The one-party state, which followed colonial rule, also inhibited artistic expression and insisted that it should conform to the party's ideology. But Zambia's artistic spirit has proved irrepressible, and its need for support has led the new government to establish an autonomous arts council funded by parliament. It provides assistance to artists, painters, sculptors, writers, and performers, and these people have made it clear they will not tolerate political interference in the council's activities.

LITERATURE AND DRAMA

Zambian literature and drama have their roots in the storytelling, song, and dance of the traditional village, but there is little surviving record of this in its authentic form. Even in recent decades very few literary works have been published, partly because of the high rates of illiteracy and poverty that restrict the market for books and partly because until 1991 the only publishers in the country were the state-owned Kenneth Kaunda Foundation and Multimedia Zambia, a firm belonging to the churches. Both kept imaginative poets and fiction writers under control.

A few novels in English have been published abroad, notably Dominic Mulaisho's *Tongue of the Dumb* (1971). Fiction in local languages has largely been confined to texts suitable for use in schools. A few biographies, such as Goodwin B. Mwangilwa's *Harry Mwaanga Nkumbula* (1982), and books on Zambian history have appeared.

The highly acclaimed novel, *Bitterness*, by Malama Katulwende was published in English in the United States in 2005. It passionately and poetically describes the clash of old African traditions and modern life in today's Zambia. An entirely different point of view is seen in the memoir *Don't Let's Go to the Dogs Tonight: An African Childhood* (2002) by Alexandra Fuller, a white British woman who was raised in war-torn southern Africa. Parts of her story take place in Zambia.

There have been two major influences on the development of theater in Zambia. One is the oral tradition of storytelling, which has led to a widespread

preference for what is seen and heard over what has to be read from the page. Another has been the British love of amateur theatricals, which led to the establishment by whites of theater clubs in Lusaka, along the Copperbelt, and elsewhere, often with a proper auditorium and the facilities needed for stage performances. After independence these theaters came under the control of Zambians, and the heritage of the stage play has lived on. The University of Zambia Theater, the Zambia National Theater Arts Association, and others promote theater extensively. Schools, colleges, universities, and even the defense forces have drama groups, while parallel to the growth of established theaters a number of clubs sprang up that rejected the British touch in favor of a postcolonial African approach to drama.

An outdoor library in Luangwa National Park features a place for tea in the shade of a large mahogany tree.

WOMEN IN ART

Women artists face more difficulties than men because the idea of female independence conflicts with traditional values and disrupts the age-old social hierarchy in which women were expected to marry and become housewives. The village division of labor made women responsible for making domestic items such as pots, baskets, and mats, but though these were often works of art in themselves, their manufacture was seen as an element of household life and not as individual expression.

Although women today have as much right to an education in the arts as men, very few have made a mark as painters or sculptors. Men in general can accept a woman working—as a book illustrator, for example—but are opposed to their finding self-realization through artistic creation outside the traditional structures. Husbands find it particularly objectionable for wives to "exhibit" themselves on the stage, and most of Zambia's actresses are single.

Female musicians, singers, and dancers face even stronger opposition and have reacted by forming a pressure group called Women in Music, to strive for the right to follow the career that suits their talents. Women's position in the arts will become more prominent as they thrust themselves out of the constraints imposed by men who act as if the attitudes of the Victorian age in Britain should prevail forever.

In 2016, Esther Lungu, the first lady of Zambia, (right) publicly extolled the participation of women in the arts at the opening of a women's art exhibit in Lusaka. She said there were no limits on how women could communicate and what media they could use to express themselves. If the country was to grow, she added, women needed to be involved in all sectors of the economy.

Plays by Zambian dramatists often deal with social problems (divorce and the laws of inheritance, for example) or historical topics, as in A. S. Masiye's *Lands of Kazembe* (1973). Playwrights and performers are often recruited to tour the country to present didactic plays as part of campaigns against, for example, AIDS.

CRAFTS

Even in the remotest villages, manufactured goods such as enamel saucepans and plastic buckets are replacing traditional craft items. In the urban areas the replacement is almost total. The craft heritage of Zambia's traditional culture is not, however, being allowed to fade away.

In the 1930s, the Livingstone Museum was founded with the express objective of collecting and preserving what in those days was called ethnological material. The museum today has as fine a collection as anywhere

The Livingstone Museum is the largest and oldest museum in Zambia.

Artisans at the
Kabwata Cultural
Village offer a
wide array of
inexpensive
handicrafts to
tourists and
locals alike.

else in Africa. Since independence, other museums have enlarged the national collection, including the Moto Moto Museum in Mbala in the north, the Nayuma Museum in the west, and the Tonga Museum in the south.

The Zambian National Arts Council manages centers where the skills to make the crafts are kept alive. In Lusaka, the Kabwata Cultural Village maintains the resources for men and women to make traditional items for sale. The museums also encourage the production of such objects and buy them for resale. Foreigners—residents in Zambia as well as tourists—buy most of the crafts. This market is also tapped by private entrepreneurs through shops in the major centers. Popular items are baskets, patterned reed mats, carved wooden bowls, baked-clay pots, masks, shields, metalwares, and musical instruments such as drums, hand pianos, and xylophones. There is considerable production of carved and polished wooden animals, birds, and human figurines.

A modern urban craft is the making of model bicycles, cars, and aircraft, usually with moving parts, using steel or aluminum wire. Model bicycles

THE HENRY TAYALI CENTER

The greatest Zambian artist of the modern period was the painter and sculptor Henry Tayali (1943–1987). Much of Tayali's work depicted the crowdedness of city life and the wish of the soul to transcend it.

The one-party state drew up a policy on the arts intended to bind artists into a "socialist-realist" straitjacket, the kind imposed by Stalin in the Soviet Union, but Zambian artists revolted and founded their own Visual Arts Council (now part of the National Arts Council) to assert their independence. With the help of well-wishers, the council acquired premises for a workshop and gallery in Lusaka, which has become the focus of activity in the visual arts. It is now called the Henry Tayali Center.

have riders whose legs move up and down as if pedaling when the machine is propelled forward. These ingenious and skillfully made toys are often the work of children.

VISUAL ARTS

Traditional baskets, mats, woodcarvings, masks, decorated pottery, jewelry, metal spearheads, combs, and axes were often of great beauty and made with a high degree of skill. But most such works were utilitarian in purpose. The concept of visual art as a means of individual, rather than communal, creative expression is relatively new in Zambia.

Some Christian missionaries, if not the more puritanical churches, wanted devotional woodcarvings and statues as well as paintings for their buildings,

A wildlife artist paints a scene on Lion Plain in South Luangwa National Park.

and this gave an opening to individual talents. In addition, Western secular education regards art as an essential part of the curriculum.

An art school was established in Lusaka shortly before independence, followed by the Department of Fine Arts at the University of Zambia, where people who chose to be artists or who have a passion for modern arts can receive training. Since then Zambia has produced dozens of fine painters and sculptors, some of them, however, self-taught. Many of these artists' works are described as social commentary, particularly on the unequal distribution of wealth in the country or the trials of urban life in contrast to the simplicity of the rural past.

Few Zambian visual artists can earn a reliable living from their work alone. While some artists are well known and popular, there are few art galleries in the country that might provide the outlets they need and few private Zambian collectors. Some artists sell their work from door to door; others exhibit in hotels and even private residences. Painters and sculptors who keep up with trends may be fortunate enough to get commissions from banks and other corporations. Despite the difficulties, which include the high cost of materials, Zambia's visual artists are producing an impressive variety of work. Henry Tayali was a famous Zambian painter whose visual art legacy lives on at the Henry Tayali Center, in Lusaka's Show Grounds, which promotes young artists. *Art in Zambia*, a book by Gabriel Ellison published in 2004, was the first to give a comprehensive history of the visual arts in Zambia. Individual talents differ, but the artists' creations are a mirror of the society as well as an expression of the individual genius.

MUSIC AND DANCE

Traditional instruments are still played throughout Zambia, although Western instruments are popular, particularly among the young. The most widely used musical instruments in Zambia are drums, which range in height from 1.5 feet (0.5 m) to 5 feet (1.5 m) and can be as wide as the diameter of the tree trunk from which they were made. Drums in a sequence of sizes form a percussion orchestra to accompany singing and dance. Drumming plays an important part of rituals, celebrations, and community interactions.

Another instrument that can be large and impressive is the *silimba* (see-leem-bah), a xylophone-type instrument. The keys are flat wooden strips tied to a wooden frame with gourd resonators, one beneath each key, in a succession of declining sizes from one end to the other. The keys are tuned to either an eight- or a five-note scale, the former close to that which

Village women of Kawaza greet visitors with song and dance around a bonfire.

characterizes much Western music, and are struck with a rod topped with a ball of rubber.

The hand piano used to be a popular solo instrument. It features iron keys mounted on a small board, which is sometimes hollowed to form a resonator. The keys are adjustable so that they can be tuned. The hand piano is held between the hands and played with the thumbs. Today the homemade guitar, constructed with a tin can as resonator, is more often heard than the hand piano.

Other traditional instruments include rattles, reed flutes, horns, rasps, and the one-string harp. All the traditional instruments are used and taught at Maramba Cultural Village in Livingstone and accompany the National Dance Troupe, which performs on state occasions and entertains at hotels and concerts.

Traditionally dance formed part of ritual ceremonies, and much of the dancing seen today has been adapted for the general audience.

Traditional singing is in choral form, with a lead voice to which the chorus responds. Solo singing, in the Western sense, is an innovation. Modern Zambian popular music, where the old instruments have given way to electric guitars, synthesizers, and factory-made drum sets, is still basically choral as far as the singing is concerned. Individual star performers are rare. Among the young, American and British pop has more following than modern Zambian music. Zambian bands are strongly influenced by Western fashion. A characteristic of the Zambian audience is that it likes its music to be played very loud. Musical tastes reflect the influence of the West and the rest of Africa.

Chisha Folotiya, founder of Mondo Music Records, which produces some of Zambia's most popular musicians, explains, "Like their predecessors in the 1970s who adapted rock and roll to a Zambian flavor and called it Zamrock, our young artists and producers have interpreted the music they have grown up with—R&B, rap, and reggae, for example—and have given it a local twist."

In big towns, nightclubs and shebeens belt the sounds of *kwela* (kwair-lah) and rumba, and many local bands play to the taste of the increasingly westernized youth. Lusaka has its own theater, the Lusaka Playhouse, featuring a variety of local Zambian productions. As part of a shopping complex built near Manda Hill in early 2004, Lusaka has a modern five-screen cinema multiplex, along with a bowling alley and a 200-seat theater that hosts local and regional cultural and musical events.

INTERNET LINKS

http://www.environmentafrica.org/2011/11/zambia-showcases-the-diverse-talents-of-local-artists-and-crafts-people
This article highlights the work of Zambian craftswomen.

https://hyperallergic.com/53287/a-secret-heritage-modern-art-in-zambia
The site offers a good article on Zambia's modern artists.

https://www.musicinafrica.net
Music in Africa covers the music scene across the continent and provides audio links for many artists. Search for Zambia to find many up-to-date articles relevant to today's music in Zambia.

https://www.musicinafrica.net/magazine/traditional-music-zambia
This site provides an overview of Zambian traditional music.

https://theculturetrip.com/africa/zambia/articles/malama-katulwende-a-zambian-literary-voice
An essay about Zambian writer Malama Katulwende is on this site.

http://www.times.co.zm/?p=86275
This opinion piece in the *Times of Zambia* argues for a true African literary tradition and the teaching of African literature in Zambian schools.

LEISURE

An experienced kayaker prepares to tackle the rapids in the Zambezi River in Livingstone.

11

I N THE REMOTE AREAS OF ZAMBIA, people make their own entertainment. Without electricity, which is usually the case in the rural regions, there's no TV, internet, or movie theaters. Everyday work—or leisure—can be enlivened with singing and dancing, while weddings are often the greatest opportunity to eat, drink, and have a good time. Local festivals to celebrate the harvest or commemorate the ancestral spirits are enjoyable occasions, but the most regular form of entertainment is storytelling around the fire at night.

People in the cities have a wider range of choices, but much depends on how much disposable income they have. Those who cannot afford to join sports clubs or other Western-style diversions are in much the same position as the rural poor, whose choices are limited.

Cinemas are located in the city centers. Enterprising people in the townships who are fortunate enough to have electricity establish their own mini-cinemas in their houses with a television set and a video player.

The Zambian soccer team celebrates after winning the African Cup of Nations Under 20 Championship in 2017.

POPULAR SPORTS

SOCCER Zambians, rich and poor, urban and rural, are united across all barriers by a passionate interest in soccer (also called football). For anyone who can scrape together enough cash, a radio—used to listen to soccer broadcasts—is as much a household item as a cooking pot. The fortunes of the national squad are followed with almost religious devotion.

Soccer is one of the sports in which Zambia excels. The game was brought to the country by the British and was promoted by the mining companies as a recreation for their workers. The earliest teams bore the names of mines, such as Bancroft Blades and Mufulira Blackpool. Over the years, other business organizations encouraged the formation of their own soccer clubs, and the sport has now reached the stage where Zambia has a full-fledged professional league. Many players who have become stars in Zambia

are taken on by clubs abroad, in Europe, Saudi Arabia, South America, and South Africa. At home the game is governed by the Football Association of Zambia (FAZ) and internationally by the Federation of International Football Associations (FIFA).

It is from this environment that the country's national team is drawn, and that team is highly regarded in Africa. In 2012, it won the Africa Cup of Nations, the football championship of Africa organised by the Confederation of African Football (CAF). Though it has yet to qualify for the World Cup, it has been close to doing so several times since 1974.

Zambia also produced Africa's most famous soccer commentator, Dennis Liwewe (1936—2014), who since the 1970s was the role model for others in the profession in many countries as a result of his broadcasts on the BBC.

Zambia may be among the best in soccer, but it is a poor country. The football association is always short of money for the development of the

Children pose with their tattered playground ball in Lusaka.

SOCCER—DISASTER AND RESURGENCE

When the Zambian national team won the 2012 Africa Cup of Nations, they dedicated their win to the members of the national team who died in a plane crash near the final's venue in Libreville in 1993.

That year, the Zambian national team was well placed to get into the finals of the 1994 World Cup. On April 27, 1993, they took off from Lusaka in a military aircraft to fly to Dakar for a qualifying match against Senegal. But the team never arrived. Immediately after leaving Libreville, Gabon, after a refueling stop the plane plunged into the sea. Eighteen players, twelve officials, and the entire aircrew perished, and Zambia lost the best soccer team it had ever had, including its captain, Wisdom Chansa.

When the news reached Zambia the next morning, people were so stunned that they shut down their offices, and crowds of mourners were seen weeping in the streets. But Zambian soccer has an inextinguishable spirit of its own, and within weeks a new team had been

formed, with Kalusha Bwalya, a Zambian soccer star playing for a Dutch club, as captain.

Against all odds, Bwalya's team came within an ace of qualifying for the 1994 World Cup and winning the African Nations Cup. It was acknowledged to be the best team in Africa. It was as if the genius of the lost team had come back from the dead.

In Zambia donations from the public generated a large sum of money to provide for the families of those who had died in Gabon. The remains of the crash victims were buried adjacent to the Independence Stadium in Lusaka, and a memorial was erected. It has become a place of pilgrimage, and visiting teams go there to pay homage to the dead before their matches in the stadium.

game, and the state's contribution to sport as a whole is small. The game extends from its central venue, the Independence Stadium in Lusaka, to every corner of the country, and Zambia also has one of the first women's leagues in Africa. Indisputably the national sport, soccer is played even by the barefooted, if only with a ball made of a bag stuffed with straw.

GOLF Another favored national game is golf, but only the wealthier folks can afford to play. Like soccer, golf was introduced by the British to the mining towns and the administrative centers. It was for decades a pastime that could be enjoyed only by whites on the many splendid links in the Copperbelt, in Lusaka, and elsewhere.

But shortly before independence, it was a Zambian, David Phiri, who became the first African to play golf for Oxford University in England and won the acclaimed status of a Blue, a top sports honor. When he returned home to work for the mines, the "color bar" crumbled. The game was given

Men play golf at the Royal Livingstone Golf Club in Livingstone. Although the course was built for British colonists, it fell into disrepair and no longer attracts tourists. Local people now play there.

Radio or wireless, which is known in the vernacular as wayaleshi *(wah-yair-lair-shee), has held an important place in the life of the country since World War II, when Zambian troops were serving in distant lands. At the time, communications within Zambia were poor, and many of the soldiers' families were unable to read. To keep the soldiers' loved ones informed of the progress of the war and of their men in arms, the government decided to distribute radios to the villages and to the community centers in the towns. But standard radio sets were large, fragile, and expensive, making distribution and upkeep difficult. The problem seemed insoluble until an information officer named Harry Franklin came up with a brilliant idea. In conjunction with the Eveready battery company in England, he designed a simple dry-cell battery set whose valves, circuits, and speaker fitted inside a small, tough saucepan.*

The saucepan sets were distributed all over the country, and at the same time Franklin set up Zambia's first broadcasting station in a Nissen hut at the airport in Lusaka. This was the beginning of the Zambia National Broadcasting Corporation (ZNBC), which covers the country with two shortwave channels, two medium-wave channels, and one FM channel. ZNBC also runs public-TV stations that broadcast only from 5 p.m. to midnight and one television channel. Since 1991, three independent radio stations have also come on the air. Zambia's addiction to radio goes back a long time, and the original saucepan radios have become collector's items.

another boost when it was taken up by President Kaunda. He laid out a nine-hole course in the spacious and elegant grounds of the president's official residence, the State House.

The presidential links are still maintained and used mainly for prestigious charitable fund-raising tournaments. Zambia, with first-class golf courses in the main population centers, is on the international golfing circuit, and thousands of Zambians play the game regularly. Even small provincial towns have golfing facilities.

BOXING AND OTHER SPORTS Boxing has a large following, too—including among women. Zambia has produced three Commonwealth Boxing Council champions—Lottie Mwale (light heavyweight), Chisanda Mutti

(cruiserweight), and Joe Sichula (heavyweight). Zambia also has a female boxing champion in Esther Phiri, who took the Women International Boxing Federation super featherweight title in 2007. In other athletics, the hurdler Samuel Matete won a bronze in the 1996 Olympics.

Zambians also swim and play tennis, squash, hockey, rugby, and bowls—a game usually played on grass with large wooden balls. For those with a taste for adventure, whitewater rafting down the Zambezi Gorges below Victoria Falls makes the adrenaline flow, as does stalking big game as a licensed hunter in one of Zambia's game management areas.

CHESS Amon Simutowe, of Mbala, Zambia, is the first grandmaster of the World Chess Federation from sub-Saharan Africa, and only the third black chess grandmaster in history. In the 2007 Euwe Stimulus Tournament, held

White-water rafters brave the rapids on the Zambezi River under the Victoria Falls.

Friends pose in the doorway of a local tavern in Rufunsa.

in Arnhem, the Netherlands, Simutowe earned his third grandmaster and was awarded the International Grandmaster title. In 2009, he won the South African chess Open. He holds a Bachelor of Science in economics and finance from the University of Texas at Dallas and a Master of Science in economics for development from the University of Oxford.

RELAXING

A favorite way for Zambians to pass the time is, quite simply, conversation. Zambians are sociable people who enjoy storytelling, and perhaps having a beer or two. In the village, the traditional meeting place is the *bwalo*. In urban areas, the tavern replaces the *bwalo*. Missionaries and the colonial government tried, with some success, to turn Zambians into teetotalers, or at least to keep "European" liquor out of their reach. For many years the only legal public drinking places in urban areas were so-called beer halls, usually owned by the local council. They were designed along the lines of a village social center, and the only liquor available was traditional beer marketed as Chibuku or Shake-Shake. After independence, beer halls were renamed taverns and continued to flourish.

Bars serve a variety of drinks. The most popular drink is bottled lager. Bars range in quality from cramped shacks in the townships to expensive "pleasure resorts" surrounded by gardens with thatched shelters against sun or rain. There is usually music from a stereo deck and on weekends a live band. People dance and may buy a meal of grilled steak, chicken, or sausages at a barbecue.

For people with money to burn, there are more-expensive pleasure centers in the cities, where they can find everything from casinos with roulette and blackjack to video games and strobe-lit dance floors.

Of all the electronic media, however, radio is the most popular, especially since the advent of the relatively cheap transistor run on batteries. A radio-cassette player can blast out music any time, and it is not unusual in the remotest places to see a herdsman tending his livestock with a radio on his shoulder. Crowds gather around a radio set when a soccer match is being broadcast, and if its owner is a budding entrepreneur he may charge a small fee for listening.

Many people listen to foreign broadcasts in English. Radio South Africa, the Voice of America, and the British Broadcasting Corporation are popular, while the Netherlands, France, Germany, Japan, and Russia also have English-language services broadcast in Zambia.

Internet cafes are sprouting up throughout Zambia, offering farmers and students connection to the web. In 2016, about four million people—one quarter of the population—had internet access.

Literate Zambians love reading, and many buy at least one newspaper a day. Sports, politics, and scandals are the most popular features, and someone will always be seen solving the crossword puzzle. Every newspaper has one, for solving crossword puzzles is another national obsession. Zambia's public libraries are few and far between, and new books are rare, but the libraries are always full of readers. Few Zambians buy books, because they are very expensive.

INTERNET LINKS

http://www.aljazeera.com/indepth/features/2016/08/zambia-rising-queens-boxing-ring-160821075942118.html
This article looks at the rising popularity of boxing among Zambian women.

http://www.espn.com/espn/eticket/story?page=phiri
ESPN provides an in-depth portrait of boxing champion Esther Phiri.

FESTIVALS

Costumed dancers perform during a celebration of the fiftieth anniversary of Zambian independence.

ZAMBIANS ENJOY A LIVELY MIX OF annual secular, national, religious, and traditional festivals and ceremonies. Some, such as the Christian holidays of Christmas and Easter, reflect the European influence on the Zambian culture. Others, primarily the traditional ceremonies, are celebrations of tribal heritage that predate the colonial era.

On the national calendar, Independence Day, October 24, is the most important event of the year. Throughout the republic it is marked with parades, and special sporting events. Labor Day, May 1, is celebrated with parades organized by the trade unions. It has become a tradition for employers to present service awards to workers on this day.

The first Monday of August is Farmers' Day, and the Zambia Agricultural and Commercial Show is held in Lusaka over that weekend. The show offers a fine display of Zambia's achievements in the farming sector and is a shop window for industrial products, with many Zambian and foreign exhibitors. The show is usually inaugurated by the president or a visiting foreign dignitary, who presents trophies to the prize winners in categories that range from Best Beef Bull to Best Industrial Stand. The show is also a great occasion for fun, with a military band, equestrian displays, and other entertainment. The Zambia International Trade Fair, held at Ndola in the Copperbelt in July, also offers a weekend of entertainment, apart from the serious business conducted between Zambian businesspeople and the worldwide exhibitors.

12

Although Christmas is an important Christian holiday, it's not celebrated in Zambia in a big way. For one thing, most Zambians are too poor to indulge in the excesses of the holiday's secular side. Western-style decorations are displayed in some commercial areas, but many Zambians complain that those European traditions are alien to their own culture.

A sanctuary worker at South Luangwa national Park dons a Santa beard and hat during the Christmas holiday season.

The most important festival on Zambia's Christian calendar is Christmas. It is the time for the exchange of greeting cards and gifts, and some churches, such as the Anglican Cathedral in Lusaka, host a charming carol-by-candlelight ceremony. Most industries in Zambia close from Christmas Eve until after New Year's Day, making this a holiday period. Christmas is increasingly commercialized in the style of Western consumer societies.

Although not designated public holidays, the Diwali of Hindus and the Eid al-Fitr of Muslims are celebrated by these communities.

TRADITIONAL CEREMONIES

Many Zambian groups hold an annual festival to celebrate their identities and to commemorate the heroes of the past who are now in the spirit world. Some of these ceremonies were suppressed during the colonial period on the grounds that they were heathen, subversive, or both. Under the one-party state, the ceremonies were controlled on the pretext that they encouraged "tribalism."

Since 1991 many of them have been publicly revived. Some are small, intimate affairs, others large and spectacular. They may be particular to one group but are now regarded as national occasions. Of those, Kuomboka of the Lozi, N'cwala of the Ngoni, Likumbilya Mize of the Luvale, Mutomboko of the Lunda, and Shimunenga of the Ila are the most outstanding. Zambians of all groups, foreign residents, and tourists are welcome to attend and do so in large numbers.

KUOMBOKA *Kuomboka* (koo-orhm-borh-kah) means "to come out of the water" and signifies the greatest public ceremony of the Lozi, the heartland

of whose kingdom is the floodplain of the Upper Zambezi. The *litunga* has two capitals, one at Lealui on the plain and another at Limulunga, on rising land on the east bank of the river. The *litunga* and his court split the year between the two palaces. In March or April, when the rainy season has run its course, the plain becomes completely flooded, and Lealui is isolated. The *litunga* must then leave there to go to Limulunga.

At the appropriate time, the royal drums are sounded, preparations are made, and the *litunga* proceeds to the royal barge, the Nalikwanda. Propelled by skilled paddlers wearing scarlet berets, the great barge crosses the floodwaters and docks at Nayuma, the harbor on the shore. Crossing the water, the Nalikwanda is followed by smaller royal barges and a flotilla of canoes.

The Lozi king crosses the swamp on board a special boat during a ceremony of the Kuomboka festival.

The music of drums, xylophones, and singers accompanies the *litunga*'s procession, and his subjects wear their traditional Lozi costume, with its brightly colored long skirts. When the *litunga* enters the Nalikwanda at Lealui he is dressed in his traditional robes, but during the journey he changes into a replica of the British admiral of the fleet uniform, which was presented to his ancestor, Lewanika, when he attended the coronation of King Edward VII in London in 1902.

The origins of Kuomboka are hidden in the past, but the ceremony as it now exists, though with a less grand barge, probably began during the reign of Litunga Mulambwa in the 1820s. This was before the English started celebrating Christmas with Christmas trees. Kuomboka can be interpreted as the symbolic annual rebirth of the Lozi kingdom by its passage through water.

The days of the ceremony are a time of feasting for the Lozi and their guests, but the ceremony is not held if the Zambezi fails to flood because of drought.

LIKUMBI LYA MIZE Mize is the place high up on the Zambezi Plain where the Luvale royal chief, or *ndungu*, has his palace and occupies a throne guarded by statues of lions. Likumbilya Mize means "the Day (in celebration of) Mize." The festival is held in September, the start of the planting season.

On that day, grounds near the palace become an arena where subordinate Luvale chiefs gather in splendid regalia to await the arrival of the ndungu, whose throne has been put in position at the head of the arena. Around the arena traditional Luvale artifacts are exhibited to remind people of their heritage. Baskets, knives, holsters, and other crafts are exhibited, but the pride of place goes to the *lutengo* (loo-tairn-gorh), a working model of an ancient iron smelter, with demonstrations by a blacksmith in the art of making hoes and arrowheads.

As the crowd waits, the arena is invaded by *makishi* (ma-kee-shee), dancers wearing elaborate brightly painted masks and tight-fitting costumes woven from different colored fibers. They represent the spirits and act out the history of the Luvale in dance with a thrilling display of gymnastics, accompanied by the insistent beating of drums.

When the time is right, the ndungu, wearing his crown and ceremonial robes, is carried in the royal hammock from the palace to the throne. The crowd pushes forward to catch a glimpse of him because by tradition he lives in seclusion in the palace. When he is seated, a headman, his body decorated in red and ochre and wearing a headdress of bright feathers, performs the royal dance *kutopoka* (koo-torh-porh-kah). The festival's climax comes as the court bard chants the history of the royal family, urging the spirits to assist the chief and pledging the loyalty of his people.

MUTOMBOKO *Mutomboko* (moo-torhm-borh-korh) means "victory dance," and it is also the name of a festival celebrated by the Lunda of the *mwata kazembe*, whose territory lies along the Luapula River in northern Zambia. Approximately three centuries ago the first mwata kazembe broke away from the Lunda empire of the mwatayamvo and crossed the Luapula River from the west into what is now Zambia, fighting and subordinating the people

A Lunda woman covers her skin in a white powder called ulupemba during ceremonies of the Mutomboko festival.

who stood in his way. The mwata kazembe's capital, the town of Kazembe (also called Mwansabombwe), lies beside the Ngona River, a tributary of the Luapula. Mutomboko is celebrated there every July 29.

The festival begins in the morning with the mwata kazembe visiting shrines and paying homage to the ancestral spirits. Priests smear him with ocher and white sacred dusts, and he proceeds to the banks of the Ngona, where he pours beer and throws food into the waters, saying, "What your fathers died for should follow you." The ritual commemorates the drowning in the Lualaba River in Congo of two of the first mwata kazembe's brothers during the migration. In the olden days, during the Mutomboko ceremony a slave was sacrificed to symbolize the mwata kazembe's victories. Today a goat is sacrificed.

Members of the royal family, chiefs, and councilors in the Lunda hierarchy wear colorful traditional costumes and take their places in an arena. A huge crowd watching the preliminary dances by girls, selected members of the royal family, and councilors surrounds them. The mwata kazembe, clad in his royal finery—modeled on a costume given to his predecessor in the eighteenth century by a Portuguese ambassador—and wearing his crown, is borne on the royal hammock into the arena amid great pomp and rejoicing.

The culmination of the ceremony comes when the mwata kazembe rises, to deafening applause, and performs the Mutomboko. He carries an axe and a sword, concluding his dance by pointing the sword to the sky (where he came from) and then to the earth (where his body will rest). He thus unites the spirits and the people in his person. The king, followed by his wildly rejoicing subjects, is then carried back to his palace.

N'CWALA   Formerly suppressed by the colonial government, *N'cwala* (in-chwah-lah) means "First Fruits and Reinvigoration" and is a festival of the once warlike Ngoni of Eastern Province. The ceremony focuses on the ruler, whose full title is Nkosiya Makosi, or King of Kings. In the past the men of the Ngoni, an offshoot of the warrior Zulus of South Africa, were organized in *impi* (eem-pee), or fighting regiments. N'cwala was the occasion for all to gather, be united through the king with the spirits, and be given renewed strength.

The ceremony, with its displays of war dancing, reaches its peak with the slaughter by hand of a black bull, which is then roasted on a spit. The king eats the first piece of cooked meat, and then all the warriors join in, the court bard chanting the praises of the monarch. At the appropriate time, the season's first fruits are presented.

N'cwala is a religious ceremony, and the ritual eating of the bull is symbolically similar to the Christian Eucharist. The *mpezeni*'s health and strength are identified with the well-being of his subjects and the fruitfulness of nature. His function at N'cwala is to bring back the departed spirits for the good of the people. The Zambian Ngoni are no longer warriors but farmers and cattle ranchers. While in the past the good of the people was achieved by conquest, today it comes from the soil, and the modern-day ceremony is most concerned with food and the prosperity its abundance assures.

Ngoni warriors known as impis perform an energetic dance during the N'cwala festival.

Today participants in N'cwala dress in the leopard skins of warriors and dance with spears and shields, ritualizing the past glories. Though the sacred bull is still eaten, so too are the first fruits of crops planted at the beginning of the rains, some four months earlier.

SHIMUNENGA The Ila of Maala in Southern Province, cattle people from the most ancient times, believe their ancestral founder to have been a leader named *Shimunenga,* who won them their territory by defeating his brother Moomba in battle. Shimunenga, after his death, did not live on as a mere spirit but as a demigod. The Ila's most sacred place is Shimunenga's *isaka* (ee-sah-kah), or holy grove, near the town of Maala. He is commemorated annually in a three-day ceremony between September and November, these pastoral people's New Year season. A direct descendant of Shimunenga, who is considered his guardian and is also a priest, decides the exact date.

The first day of the festival is the women's day. They go around the villages dancing, singing, and drinking. The songs are meant to provoke the men. On this day the men do nothing active except drink beer. On the second day the women pay homage to Shimunenga at his grove. Later everyone gathers at the palace of the chief, or *mungaila.* A sermon is given at Shimunenga's *isaka* on the lives of his people, and speeches are made, followed by singing and dancing until all are exhausted.

On the third day there is an awe-inspiring display of the Ila's best cattle. The herds, led by that of the chief, are driven in succession to singing and the beating of drums. After the roundup the celebration of well-being continues with dancing and games, which include mock battles with real spears and dramatized lion hunts. When it is all over around midday, the people having paid homage and offered thanks to Shimunenga for his beneficence, they retire to drink beer, which is also a libation to the demigod.

Spectators at the Shimunenga festival are warned that to desecrate the sacred grove by entering it can bring dire consequences.

THE LIVINGSTONE INTERNATIONAL CULTURAL ARTS FESTIVAL

One of the most exciting and fastest growing new festivals in Zambia is the Livingstone Cultural Arts Festival (LICAF) in—where else?—the historic town of Livingstone on the Zambezi River near the Victoria Falls. Begun in 2013 by the Livingstone Initiative and the Zambian Tourism Board to showcase African dance and music groups, the annual March event has quickly grown into a weekend-long pop festival, cultural panorama, and street carnival. The 2016 festival drew performers from across the globe, including dance troupes from China and India.

INTERNET LINKS

http://www.livingstoneculturalfestival.com
This is the home page of the LICAF.

http://www.mota.gov.zm/index.php/features/arts-and-culture/2012-12-22-03-04-35/traditional-ceremonies
The Ministry of Tourism and Arts posts a long list of Zambia's tribal Traditional Ceremonies.

https://www.timeanddate.com/holidays/zambia
This calendar site lists the Zambian holidays for the current year.

http://vibrant-africa.com/content/2747
This article with photos is about the Shimunenga Ceremony.

http://www.zambiatourism.com/about-zambia/people/festivals
This travel site explains the most popular Traditional Ceremonies.

FOOD

A woman fills a bucket with roasted, sun-dried caterpillars she is selling at the Soweto Market in Lusaka.

13

C ORN, OR MAIZE, WHICH WAS introduced to Africa by the Portuguese centuries ago, has become the staple food for most Zambians. Four other introduced starch crops—cassava, wheat, potatoes, and sweet potatoes— are also important. Before the arrival of these foods, the staple grains were the indigenous millet and sorghum and a little rice. Corn is ground and cooked with water to make a stiff porridge called *nshima* (in-shee-mah) or *nsima*, which can be eaten with the fingers.

WOMEN AND FOOD

Women grow most of the basic foods in Zambia. In the traditional village, a woman not only spends much time in the fields but also long hours preparing food. She has to collect firewood, carry water from the well or the stream, and turn corn into meal by pounding it in a mortar or grinding it between stones. Cassava has to be soaked in water for a week to remove the poison in it, cut into chips, and dried before it can be made into flour.

Insects such as grasshoppers, caterpillars, cicadas and flying ants are considered delicacies. During the rainy season, termites swarm in the air and can be easily caught. After pulling off their wings, the cook tosses the termites into a hot frying pan with oil and sautés them to golden brown. The crispy treats are served in a bowl like peanuts.

Women with baskets of goods wait for customers at the open-air market in Lukasa.

Today many villages have a small mechanical mill where grain is ground for a fee. In towns, factory-made meal is available in the shops, and it is even possible to buy precooked nshima that is ready to be eaten when boiling water is added to it. Nshima can be likened to the Italian polenta. Leftovers can be cut into slices, dipped in egg, and fried in oil to make fritters.

In the urban areas, women run most of the food stalls in the markets or on the street. They usually sell nshima with grilled steak, chicken, or sausages, though more and more townspeople eat bread from bakeries and fried potato chips. Hamburgers with French fries are popular.

Many women go into the city center to sell a tray of hard-boiled eggs, sausage rolls, deep-fried doughnuts, or roasted peanuts that they prepared at home. To a very large extent, it is the women who keep Zambia fed.

The food culture of Zambia is largely influenced by extreme poverty. How else to explain a "cuisine" in which people eat mice and insects—and, in fact, consider them tasty treats?

Despite Zambia's recent economic growth and relative political stability, its people live on the edge of starvation. The 2016 Global Hunger Index (GHI) Report ranks Zambia as the third hungriest country on earth. Only Central African Republic and Chad are worse off. Published by the International Food Policy Research Institute, the Hunger Index ranks countries based on undernourishment, child mortality, child wasting (low weight for height) and child stunting (low height for age). According to the GHI statistics, 47.8 percent of Zambians are undernourished; 6.3 percent of children under five years are wasting; 40 percent of children are stunted; and the under five mortality rate is 6.4 percent.

This level of hunger is especially shocking for a country that the World Bank classifies as "lower middle income." It's also very concerning that Zambia's GHI score has been steadily declining since 2000, and has dropped by 6.2 points since 2008.

What is hunger? There are various levels of food insufficiency, from outright starvation, which means dying of hunger; to hunger; to food insecurity, which means the lack of a regular supply of healthy food, or occasional hunger.

As understood by organizations that address the problem, hunger means far more than most people in industrialized nations can understand. The Food and Agriculture Organization of the United Nations (FAO) defines food deprivation, or undernourishment, as "the consumption of food that is not sufficient to provide the minimum amount of dietary energy that each individual requires to live a healthy and productive life, given his or her sex, age, stature, and physical activity level."

Hunger is not only the result of an empty belly. A Zambian child can fill up on nshima, the country's staple food, and still suffer from malnourishment. A starch-heavy diet lacks essential nutrients, which, in children, can permanently impair their bodies and minds.

ZAMBIAN SPECIALTIES

If carbohydrate-rich nshima is the foundation of most Zambian meals, there are many protein foods to go with it. Those who can afford it will have beef, chicken, mutton, or pork cooked in a variety of ways. One way is to grill it over a charcoal fire in a brazier called an *mbaula* (im-bah-ool-lah). Another is in a stew containing onions and tomatoes. Herbs and spices are little used, and Zambian cuisine is generally bland.

Fish is also very popular and comes from Zambia's many rivers, lakes, and wetlands. Fresh fish is transported from its source either packed in ice or in deep-freeze trucks. Much also comes to the markets sun-dried or smoked. The most widely eaten varieties are tilapia, which is raised on fish farms as well as fished, and *kapenta*, the freshwater sardinelike fish from lakes Tanganyika and Kariba.

Other protein foods include field mice, boiled or grilled on skewers such as kebabs, and locusts, several types of grasshopper, tree caterpillars, and termites, all of which are roasted.

A dish of tilapia stew includes a scoop of nshima and greens.

The meat of wild animals such as antelope, buffalo, and hippopotamuses has always been part of the Zambian diet, but hunting is regulated and for some species is now forbidden. Such meat is now less common despite the activities of poachers. Zambia has a number of game ranches, however, with the result that venison can be found in the shops, but it is expensive. Birds such as guinea fowl, francolins, quail, doves, and pigeons also feed the pot.

Much use is made of vegetables such as cabbages, greens, and a variety of wild spinach called *libondwe* (lee-borhn-dwair), as well as okras, beans, and fresh or dried peanuts.

During the rainy season, the forests yield a bountiful crop of wild mushrooms, many of which are edible and have a unique flavor. In color they may be white, brown, scarlet, or bright yellow and may look alarming to those who have eaten only cultivated mushrooms bought in a shop. Zambians cook their mushrooms in water or with a little oil. They can be added to meat and vegetable stews, and some varieties are dried for future use. In the rural areas, they are sold along the roadside, though large quantities are brought to urban markets.

A woman carries plates of bananas.

Tropical fruit such as mangoes, pineapples, guavas, and wild plums from the forests are eaten daily when they are in season.

Many well-off Zambians have Western foods on their dining tables—cornflakes and bacon and eggs for breakfast, beans on toast as a snack, and roast chicken for dinner—but it would be unusual if nshima were not served as part of at least one meal a day.

MARKETS AND SUPERMARKETS

Evidence of how productive the soil of Zambia can be is visible all year round in the markets in urban areas. There are piles of tomatoes, onions, potatoes, cabbages, eggplants, cucumbers, pumpkins, beans, bananas, oranges, and lemons on offer. Beside the fresh-produce stalls are others selling chickens, eggs, and fresh and dried fish. Visitors from cold climates always express surprise and delight at the freshness of Zambian fruit and vegetables and the full flavor of the meat, though the freshwater fish does not have quite the tang of fish that comes from the sea.

In the brightly lit air-conditioned modern supermarkets, customers find displays of every type of food. There is a butcher's counter with beef, lamb, pork, and perhaps venison, and freezers containing chicken and locally processed bacon, ham, and other meats, as well as Nile perch, kapenta, and bream. The dairy chests hold fresh pasteurized milk and cream, Zambian butter, cheeses, yogurt, and ice cream. There are a half-dozen types of bread as well as ready-to-cook snacks such as samosas, spring rolls, and meat pies. In addition, the customer will find a wide range of imported foodstuffs—Greek olives, South African sea fish, Chinese bean sprouts.

BEVERAGES

Traditional Zambian beer is brewed from millet, sorghum, or corn. Grain is first malted by being allowed to sprout and then dried. It is pounded into meal and soaked in water to ferment in several stages. The result is a slightly fizzy alcoholic drink. This beer is now also made in factories and called Chibuku. Chibuku is also called Shake-Shake because the container must be shaken to mix the liquid and the solids.

Tea and coffee are not widely consumed, though Zambia produces tea and a fine arabica coffee, which is much in demand abroad, especially in Germany. The most popular nonalcoholic drinks are carbonated products such as Coca-Cola, Pepsi, Sprite, and Fanta. A favorite traditional nonalcoholic drink is *munkoyo*, a sweet beerlike drink named after a tuber that is its main ingredient.

TRADITIONS AND ETIQUETTE

It is not customary for Zambians to invite guests to their homes. Westerners may find this disconcerting and see it as a sign of unfriendliness. But that is not the case at all. Zambians expect friendly acquaintances to call on them unannounced.

They will be treated as honored guests and immediately offered a drink and a snack. If mealtime is approaching the visitor will be asked to join in. It is customary to cook more food than needed for the family, just in case visitors should arrive.

INTERNET LINKS

http://ghi.ifpri.org
The results of the Global Hunger Index can be found on this site.

http://www.our-africa.org/zambia/food-daily-life
This site provides some information and videos about food in Zambia and neighboring African countries.

http://www.travelingeast.com/africa/zambia/zambian-cuisine
This page takes a look at some of Zambia's more unusual foods.

https://www.wfp.org/stories/10-facts-about-hunger-zambia
The World Food Programme lists facts relating to hunger in Zambia.

IFISASHI (GREENS IN PEANUT SAUCE)

This dish is popular throughout southern Africa. It is traditionally served with nshima. The recipe is variable and exact amounts are not necessary.

1—2 cups raw (150—300 grams) peanuts, finely ground (a food processor is not traditional, but makes this step easier)
1 onion, chopped
2 tomatoes, diced
1—2 lbs (450 g) greens such as spinach, chard, kale, mustard, or collards (traditionally, pumpkin or sweet potato leaves are often used)

1—2 cups (150—300 g) chopped green cabbage (optional)
2 cups (240 milliliters) water, or more as needed.
Salt and pepper to taste

Bring water to a boil in a large pot and add the peanuts, tomatoes, and onion. Cook on high heat for several minutes, stirring often. Reduce heat to medium and stir in greens, add salt. Cover and cook for 15 minutes to an hour, stirring occasionally. (Cooking time varies by type of greens used). Add water if mixture becomes dry and starts to scorch.

Continue cooking until greens and peanuts are reduced to a thick sauce. Adjust seasonings.

NSHIMA

2 cups (320 g) finely ground white cornmeal (maize) or corn flour (not corn starch)
4 cups (950 mL) water (salted, optional)

In a large pot, bring water to a boil. Slowly add cornmeal, a little at a time, stirring continuously with a wooden spoon.

As mixture begins to bubble, reduce heat to medium and continue adding remaining cornmeal.

Stir constantly until thickened. Continue cooking over low heat for 3—4 minutes by continuing to stir the dough until it reaches the consistency of a thick, smooth, and slightly elastic dough (like soft, sticky Play-Doh).

Turn off heat, cover pot and let it site for a few minutes. Spoon into a bowl or form into large egg-shaped servings. Serve with meat, poultry, fish, or vegetables.

MEALIE BREAD (ZAMBIAN-STYLE CORNBREAD)

Mealie meal is what Zambians call cornmeal. Cornbread is popular throughout southern Africa.

1 ½ cup (250 grams) fresh or frozen corn kernels, thawed
2 eggs
1 cup (120 g) flour *and* 1 cup (160 g) cornmeal
2 tsp baking powder
2 Tbsp sugar
½ tsp paprika, 1 tsp salt
½ cup (120 mL) milk
2 Tbsp (30 g) butter, melted

Preheat oven to 350 degrees Fahrenheit (175 Celsius). Butter a loaf pan (or use baking spray). Using a food processor or blender, pulse the corn without water until it is coarsely ground. Set aside.

In a medium bowl, whisk together the flour, cornmeal, baking powder, sugar, paprika, and salt. Whisk in the milk and lightly beaten eggs until well combined. Finally, stir in the corn mixture and melted butter. Pour the batter into the prepared pan.

Bake the mealie bread for 40—45 minutes until golden brown, or until a toothpick inserted into the center comes out clean. Cool the bread in the pan for 5—10 minutes before turning the bread out onto a wire rack to continue cooling. Serve warm with butter.

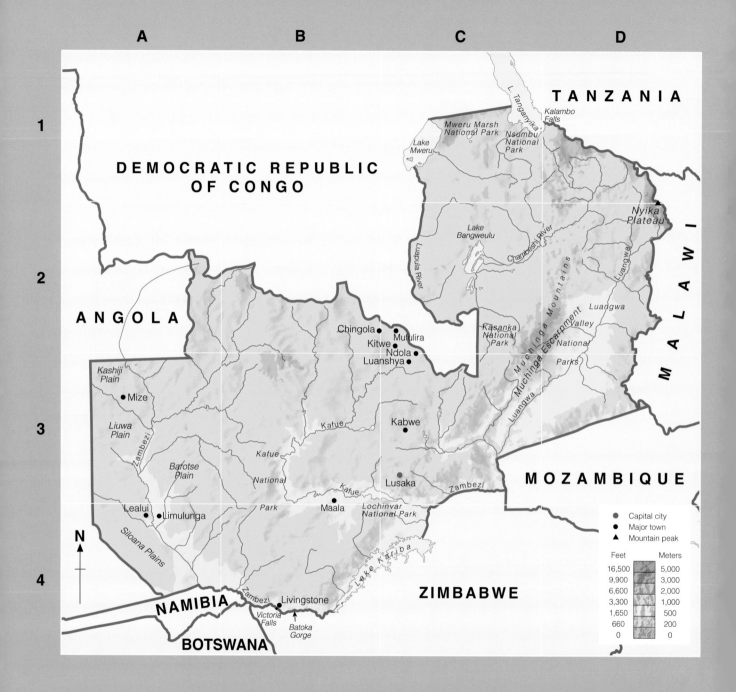

MAP OF ZAMBIA

ECONOMIC ZAMBIA

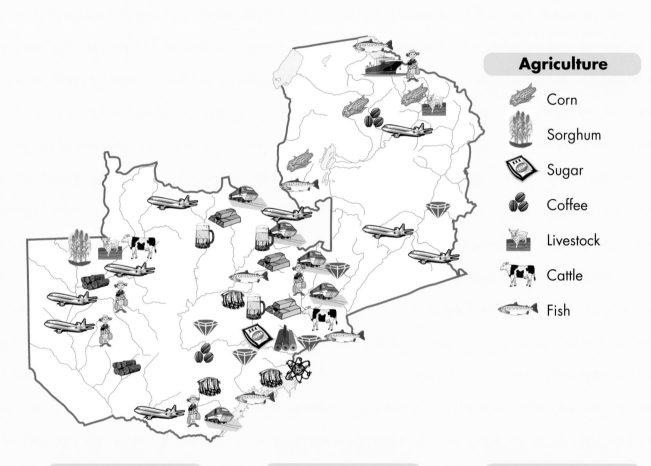

Agriculture

 Corn

 Sorghum

 Sugar

 Coffee

 Livestock

 Cattle

 Fish

Manufacturing

 Textile

 Beer

Natural Resources

 Copper and cobalt

Gemstones

Gold

Hydropower

Uranium

 Timber

Services

Airport

Port

Tourism

 Train station

ABOUT THE ECONOMY

GROSS DOMESTIC PRODUCT (GDP)
(official exchange rate)
$21.31 billion (2016 estimate)

GDP GROWTH
3 percent (2016)

GDP PER CAPITA
$3,900 (2016)

GDP BY SECTOR
Agriculture, 9.2 percent
Industry, 29.2 percent
Services, 61.7 percent (2016)

CURRENCY
Zambian kwacha (ZMK) (redenominated in 2012)
1 kwatcha = 100 ngwee
Notes: 10, 20, 50, 100, 500, 1,000 kwacha
Coins: 5, 10, 50 ngwee and 1 kwacha
1 USD = 8,917 ZMK (August 2017)

LAND USE
Agricultural land, 31.7 percent:
    arable land, 4.8 percent;
    permanent pasture, 26.9 percent
Forest, 66.3 percent
Other, 2 percent (2011)

NATURAL RESOURCES
Copper, cobalt, zinc, lead, coal, emeralds, gold, silver, uranium, and hydropower

AGRICULTURAL PRODUCTS
Corn, sorghum, rice, peanuts, sunflower seeds, vegetables, flowers, tobacco, cotton, sugarcane, cassava (tapioca), coffee, cattle, goats, pigs, milk, eggs, and hides

INDUSTRIES
Copper mining and processing, emerald mining, construction, foodstuffs, beverages, chemicals, textiles, fertilizer, horticulture

MAJOR EXPORTS
Copper, cobalt, electricity, tobacco, flowers, and cotton

MAJOR IMPORTS
Machinery, transportation equipment, petroleum products, electricity, fertilizer, foodstuffs, and clothing

MAIN TRADE PARTNERS
South Africa, Switzerland, China, United Kingdom, Zimbabwe, Democratic Republic of Congo, Mauritius, Kenya, and India

WORKFORCE
7.116 million (2016)

UNEMPLOYMENT RATE
13.3 percent (2014)

POPULATION BELOW POVERTY LINE
60.5 percent (2010)

CULTURAL ZAMBIA

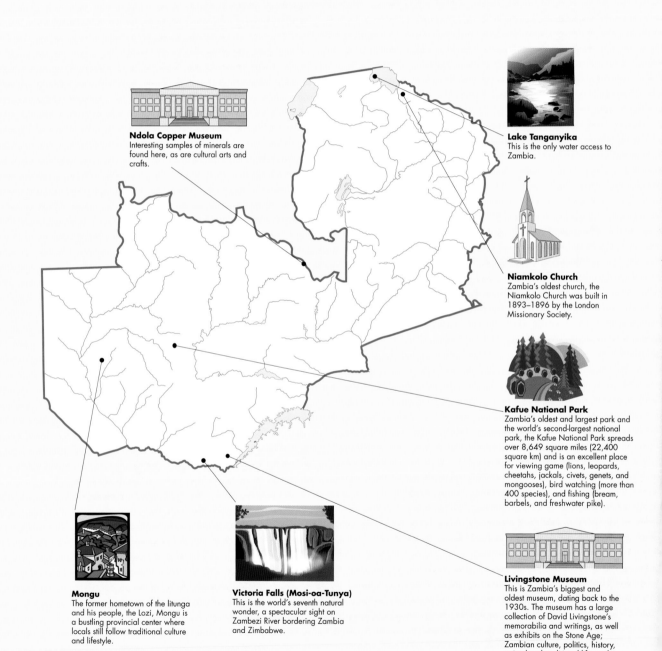

Ndola Copper Museum
Interesting samples of minerals are found here, as are cultural arts and crafts.

Lake Tanganyika
This is the only water access to Zambia.

Niamkolo Church
Zambia's oldest church, the Niamkolo Church was built in 1893–1896 by the London Missionary Society.

Kafue National Park
Zambia's oldest and largest park and the world's second-largest national park, the Kafue National Park spreads over 8,649 square miles (22,400 square km) and is an excellent place for viewing game (lions, leopards, cheetahs, jackals, civets, genets, and mongooses), bird watching (more than 400 species), and fishing (bream, barbels, and freshwater pike).

Mongu
The former hometown of the litunga and his people, the Lozi, Mongu is a bustling provincial center where locals still follow traditional culture and lifestyle.

Victoria Falls (Mosi-oa-Tunya)
This is the world's seventh natural wonder, a spectacular sight on Zambezi River bordering Zambia and Zimbabwe.

Livingstone Museum
This is Zambia's biggest and oldest museum, dating back to the 1930s. The museum has a large collection of David Livingstone's memorabilia and writings, as well as exhibits on the Stone Age; Zambian culture, politics, history, animal and traditional life, and witchcraft; and sculpture and paintings by local artists.

ABOUT THE CULTURE

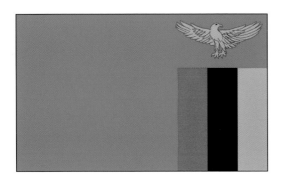

OFFICIAL NAME
Republic of Zambia

GOVERNMENT TYPE
Presidential republic

NATIONAL SYMBOLS
African fish eagle; national colors—green, red, black, orange

CAPITAL
Lusaka

POPULATION
15,510,700 (2016)

ETHNIC GROUPS
Bemba 21 percent, Tonga 13.6 percent, Chewa 7.4 percent, Lozi 5.7 percent, Nsenga 5.3 percent, Tumbuka 4.4 percent, Ngoni 4 percent, Lala 3.1 percent, Kaonde 2.9 percent, Namwanga 2.8 percent, Lunda 2.6 percent, Mambwe 2.5 percent, Luvale 2.2 percent, Lamba 2.1 percent, Ushi 1.9 percent, Lenje 1.6 percent, Bisa 1.6 percent, Mbunda 1.2 percent, other 13.8

percent, unspecified 0.4 percent (2010)

RELIGIONS
Protestant 75.3 percent, Roman Catholic 20.2 percent, other 2.7 percent, none 1.8 percent (2010)

LANGUAGES
Bembe 33.4 percent, Nyanja 14.7 percent, Tonga 11.4 percent, Lozi 5.5 percent, Chewa 4.5 percent, Nsenga 2.9 percent, Tumbuka 2.5 percent, Lunda 1.9 percent, Kaonde 1.8 percent, Lala 1.8 percent, Lamba 1.8 percent, English (official) 1.7 percent, Luvale 1.5 percent, Mambwe 1.3 percent, Namwanga 1.2 percent, Lenje 1.1 percent, Bisa 1 percent, other 9.7 percent, unspecified 0.2 percent. (2010)

BIRTHRATE
41.8 births per 1,000 Zambians (2016)

DEATH RATE
12.4 deaths per 1,000 Zambians* (2016)

INFANT MORTALITY RATE
62.9 deaths per 1,000 live births* (2016)

LIFE EXPECTANCY AT BIRTH
52.5 years* (2016)

LITERACY RATE
63.4 percent (2015)
Male, 70.9 percent
Female, 56 percent

*Estimates take into account the excess mortality in this country due to AIDS.

TIMELINE

IN ZAMBIA	IN THE WORLD
1600–1800 CE Migrating Bantu-speaking people push out original San inhabitants.	**1620 CE** Pilgrims sail the *Mayflower* from England to America. **1776** American colonies declare independence from Britain.
1851 British missionary David Livingstone visits.	**1869** The Suez Canal opens.
1889 Britain gains controls of Northern Rhodesia.	
	1914–1919 World War I
Late 1920s Discovery of extensive copper deposits.	
1935 Colonial government makes Lusaka capital of Northern Rhodesia.	
1939 Zambia becomes a major producer of copper; attracts European settlers.	**1939–1945** World War II
1953–1963 Northern Rhodesian, Southern Rhodesia, and Nyasaland are a federation.	**1949** NATO is formed.
1964 Zambia gains independence from Britain; Kenneth Kaunda is the first president.	**1966–1976** The Chinese Cultural Revolution
1972 Zambia becomes a one-party state under UNIP.	**1969** US astronaut Neil Armstrong becomes the first human to walk on the moon.
1980s and 1990s Declining copper prices and prolonged drought hurt the economy. AIDS epidemic ravages Zambia.	**1986** Nuclear power disaster at Chernobyl in Ukraine.

IN ZAMBIA		IN THE WORLD
1991		**1991**
Frederick Chiluba is elected president. Multiparty constitution adopted.		Breakup of the Soviet Union.
		1997
2000		Hong Kong is returned to China.
Severe droughts and food shortages.		
2001–2002		**2001**
Levy Mwanawasa is elected president. Floods and droughts create a national food crisis; 4 million people face starvation		Terrorists crash planes in New York, Washington, DC, and Pennsylvania.
		2003
2007		War in Iraq begins.
High Court in Britain rules former president Frederick Chiluba and four of his aides conspired to rob Zambia of about $46 million.		
2008		**2008**
President Mwanawasa dies of a stroke.		US elects first African American president, Barack Obama.
2010		
UN shows Zambia worse off than in 1970, partly due to AIDS.		
2011		**2011**
Former President Frederick Chiluba dies. Michael Sata becomes president.		Earthquake triggers deadly tsunami in Japan.
2014		
President Sata dies.		
2015		**2015–2016**
Edgar Lungu elected president		ISIS launches terror attacks in Belgium and France.
2017		**2017**
Opposition leader Hakainde Hichilema is detained and charged with treason, after his convoy failed to stop for that of President Lungu. Forty-eight opposition MPs are suspended from parliament for boycotting an address by President Lungu.		Donald Trump becomes US president. Britain begins Brexit process of leaving the EU. Hurricane Harvey devastates Houston. Hurricane Maria destroys Puerto Rico.

GLOSSARY

Bantu
"People," also used to describe an African tribe and language

Batwa
short-statured indigenous African people, also called pygmies

bwalo (bwah-lorh)
Village meeting place

kapenta (kah-paint-ah)
Sardinelike fish

kufa (koo-fah)
Word for "to die" in several Bantu languages

Kuomboka
Lozi ceremony; literally "to come out of the water"

kwacha
Zambian currency

Lesa
In indigenous religion, the supreme creator

libondwe (lee-borhn-dwair)
Wild spinach

lobola (lorh-borh-lah)
Bride price

makishi (ma-kee-shee)
Dancers at the Likumbilya Mize festival

Mandevu
Literally, "bearded"; refers to the Zion Apostolics

mbaula (im-bah-ool-lah)
Charcoal grill

Mosi-oa-Tunya
Zambian name for Victoria Falls

munkoyo (moon-korh-yorh)
Wild tuber used in making sweet beer

Mutomboko (moo-torhm-borh-korh)
Victory dance festival of the Lunda

N'cwala (in-chwah-lah)
First Fruits and Reinvigoration festival of the Ngoni

nshima (in-shee-mah)
Thick corn porridge

shimunenga (shee-moo-nairn-gah)
Ancestral founder of the Ila of Maala

wayaleshi (wah-yair-lair-shee)
Wireless; radio set

FOR FURTHER INFORMATION

BOOKS

Fuller, Alexandra. *Don't Let's Go to the Dogs Tonight. New York:* Random House, 2003. (memoir)

Katulwende, Malama. *Bitterness*. New York: Mondial, 2005. (fiction)

McIntyre, Chris. *Zambia: The Bradt Travel Guide.* Guilford, CT: The Globe Pequot Press, 2016.

Stuart, Chris and Mathilde Stuart. *Stuarts' Field Guide to Mammals of Southern African: Including Angola, Zambia & Malawi.* Cape Town: Struik Nature, 5th edition, 2015.

Taylor, Scott D. *Culture and Customs of Zambia.* Westport, CT: Greenwood Press, 2006.

ONLINE

BBC News. Zambia country profile. http://www.bbc.com/news/world-africa-14112449

____. Zambia profile—Timeline. http://www.bbc.com/news/world-africa-14113084

Chalo Chatu.org. The Zambian Online Encyclopedia. http://chalochatu.org/Main_Page

CIA World Factbook. Zambia. https://www.cia.gov/library/publications/the-world-factbook/geos/za.html

Encyclopaedia Britannica. Zambia. https://www.britannica.com/place/Zambia

Lusakatimes. https://www.lusakatimes.com

Times of Zambia. http://www.times.co.zm

Zambia Daily Mail. https://www.daily-mail.co.zm

BIBLIOGRAPHY

BBC News. Zambia country profile. http://www.bbc.com/news/world-africa-14112449
_____Zambia profile—Timeline. http://www.bbc.com/news/world-africa-14113084

CIA World Factbook. Zambia. https://www.cia.gov/library/publications/the-world-factbook/geos/za.html

Dörrie, Peter. "The Wars Ravaging Africa in 2016." *The National Interest*, January 22, 2016. http://nationalinterest.org/blog/the-buzz/the-wars-ravaging-africa-2016-14993

Encyclopaedia Britannica. Zambia. https://www.britannica.com/place/Zambia

GLI. "Zambia: Energy 2017." Global Legal Insights. https://www.globallegalinsights.com/practice-areas/energy/global-legal-insights---energy-5th-ed./zambia

Gregson, Jonathan. "The Poorest Countries in the World." *Global Finance*, February 13, 2017. https://www.gfmag.com/global-data/economic-data/the-poorest-countries-in-the-world?page=12

Hobbes, Michael. "Why Is Zambia So Poor?" Pacific Standard, September 12, 2013. https://psmag.com/economics/zambia-poor-poverty-globalization-mining-corruption-66080

Kaunda, Danstan. "As drought hits Zambian harvests, food prices are on the rise." Reuters, September 8, 2016. http://www.reuters.com/article/us-zambia-drought-food/as-drought-hits-zambian-harvests-food-prices-are-on-the-rise-idUSKCN11E0SC

Kimenyi, Mwangi S. And Amy Copley. "The Death of President Michael Sata and Issues of the Health of African Leaders." Brookings, October 30, 2014. https://www.brookings.edu/blog/africa-in-focus/2014/10/30/the-death-of-president-michael-sata-and-issues-of-the-health-of-african-leaders

Smithsonian National Museum of Natural History. "What does it mean to be human? Kabwe 1." http://humanorigins.si.edu/evidence/human-fossils/fossils/kabwe-1

Udoh, Nse. "Go to Hell, Edgar Lungu tells Gay Rights Activists." Zambia Reports, May 21, 2013. https://zambiareports.com/2013/05/21/go-to-hell-edgar-lungu-tells-gay-rights-activists

World Bank Group. "World Bank President Praises Reforms In Zambia, Underscores Need For Continued Improvements In Policy And Governance." December 18, 2010. http://www.worldbank.org/en/news/press-release/2010/12/18/world-bank-president-praises-reforms-zambia-underscores-need-continued-improvements-policy-governance

World Bank Group. "Zambia Economic Brief: Reaping Richer Returns from Public Expenditures in Agriculture." The World Bank, June 2017. http://documents.worldbank.org/curated/en/130381498665479930/pdf/117003-WP-P157243-PUBLIC-World-Bank-9th-Zambia-Economic-Brief-June-2017-FINAL-WEB.pdf

World Population Review. "Zambia Population 2017." http://worldpopulationreview.com/countries/zambia-population

INDEX

INDEX